FROM
TO THE ARCTIC

A year on the destroyer
HMS Beagle during World War II

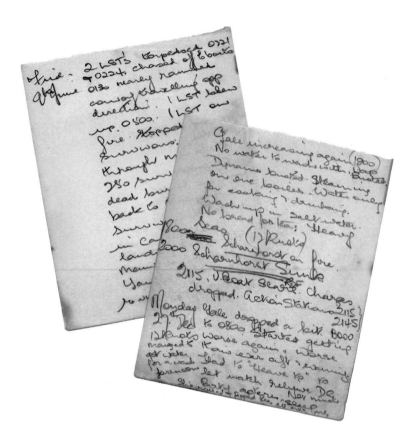

Above - Extracts from Peter Ward's original diary

Dedicated to Jean, Nicky and Sue

'Lest We Forget'

FROM AFRICA
TO THE ARCTIC

A year on the destroyer
HMS Beagle during World War II

Peter Ward

BREWIN BOOKS

First published by Brewin Books Ltd
Studley, Warwickshire B80 7LG in 2003
www.brewinbooks.com

ISBN 1 85858 237 7

British Library Cataloguing in Publication Data
A Catalogue record for this book is available from the British Library.

Typeset in Times
Printed in Great Britain
by SupaPrint (Redditch) Limited.
www.supaprint.com

CONTENTS

ILLUSTRATIONS

FOREWORD

21st March 2003

"Beagle" was the happiest of four ships I served in during WWII. Some kind spirit seemed to smile on us, saving us on all manner of occasions, particularly when combing the tracks of 2 or more incoming torpedoes.

We were blessed also with a splendid company, led by Norman Murch, who combined care for the ship and her people, with zeal and zest for inspired destroyer command. Only in other ships were there many "Captain's defaulters". In "Beagle" they were rare, respect for the "old man" and his skill in preserving us was the reason.

Leading Seaman (Radar) at 21, Peter Ward was responsible for the effectiveness of our new type 271 Surface Radar. He typifies so many of those volunteers who decided to postpone the benefits of higher education, while serving in the fleet on very active service. Postwar he has pursued a distinguished career in the world of music.

In harbour he was coxswain of the motor boat, as in the midwinter visit to the immobile Soviet destroyers at Polyarnoe. What a delicious irony that while No:1 & I were being persistently plied with tumblers (yes tumblers!) of vodka before being repeatedly questioned about the range of our 271 Radar, Peter Ward fortunately still wearing his duffle coat (thus hiding his badge), was being 'looked after' elsewhere by those who were quite unaware that Peter was our Radar expert and knew far more about it than either No:1 or I.

A strange foretaste of post war life during the 'Cold War'.

Colin McMilan

Lieut-Cdr Royal Navy
("Sub" of the "Beagle" 1943-1944).

INTRODUCTION

I cannot remember what prompted me to keep a diary for the whole of the year that I spent as a member of the crew of HMS Beagle, as opposed to my service on HMS Sweet Briar, HMS Sunk Head Fort and HMS Arbiter, all of which were engaged in activities worthy of mention.

The Diary remained unread for fifty years, in fact until the fiftieth anniversaries of the North Atlantic Convoys (Liverpool) and the 'D' Day Landings (Southsea). These occasions were responsible for my re-reading the pencilled daily records which, incidentally, were mainly factual and sometimes brief, recording the number of ships in various convoys, the speed and direction, the state of the weather, the ports of call and also describing action involving the enemy (U boats etc.).

I then felt the urge to type up the basic Diary entries, subsequently doing so several times, each time expanding them to make them more readable by digging into my memory thereby adding explanations, further thoughts and more detail. 'Jock', my friend and opposite number and fellow Leading Seaman Radar, mentioned in the text of the Diary, died many years ago and, had he lived, would have been invaluable in recalling the HMS Beagle's activities, shipmates, background etc.

As the Diary grew in content, making it of greater interest to people other than myself, and as a result of help and encouragement from my wife Jean, relatives and friends my mind turned to the possibility of finding a publisher.

After the several re-writings, I was fortunate to be given the name of Brewin Books Ltd., who agreed to publication, thus making the translation of my manuscript into the form of a book possible.

The Imperial War Museum (London) have been most helpful in providing photographs of the 'Beagle', together with pictures of convoys, the infernal weather conditions and treacherous seas, the North Atlantic environment etc., all mentioned in the text, but adding a visual aspect to the printed word. The photographs augmented my meagre collection, small naval ships not having the photographic facilities of the larger ones, such as cruisers, aircraft carriers and battleships.

I would like to think that this book will be one of many memorials to all those sailors who risked their lives for the benefit of mankind, some of them making the ultimate sacrifice. I hope that records such as this about World War II, of which there are many, will remind people of the horrors of War. I was one of the lucky ones.

FROM AFRICA TO THE ARCTIC
A YEAR ABOARD 'HMS BEAGLE' DURING
THE SECOND WORLD WAR

PREAMBLE
(Naval life before the 'Beagle')

It was a typical June morning when I first clapped eyes on what was to be my 'home of steel' for the next year. Little did I know what was in store whilst contemplating HMS Beagle on this day, 3rd.June,1943. My previous naval experience included 'joining up' at 'HMS Glendower ', Pwllheli, North Wales (a converted Butlin's holiday camp (!) taken over for the duration of the war) as an AB (Able Seaman), at the tender age of 19 years 8 months. This was followed by three weeks Radar training at Douglas, Isle of Man, where we were billeted in hotels (also adapted as naval establishments) situated on the sea front and used by holiday-makers pre-war. I must confess that the 'service' was somewhat below peace- time expectations! This was followed immediately by three months service on a 'Flower Class' corvette 'HMS Sweet Briar' as an RDF (Radio Direction Finding) rating.

It was an emergency posting, the normal operator having been taken ill, with 'Sweet Briar' being rescheduled to carry out North Atlantic patrols from an Icelandic base (Reykjavik) in search of a German Pocket Battleship! Needless to say we were unsuccessful! I ought to mention that it was on the same day our training group qualified as bona fide Radar Operators, volunteers were invited to replace the sick operator (mentioned earlier) and yours truly indicated his willingness to co-operate. Our group was under the mistaken impression that 'Sweet Briar' was due to sail to America. That was the 'buzz' (rumour) and nothing could have been further from the truth! I must have been very naïve! I think it fair to say that my life on HMS Sweet Briar was short but not very sweet. Leaving 'Sweet Briar', and following a brief sojourn at one of His Majesty's free hotels (I think it was the Portsmouth base, HMS Victory), I joined HMS Sunk Head Fort in April 1942, spending a year 'Boxing and Coxing', alternating service on the Fort and home leave which was, as far as I can remember, four weeks on the fort and two weeks ashore.

The Fort consisted of two concrete towers with a concrete base, resting on a sandbank off the East Coast – our base was Harwich – straddled by a metal deck on which was a main gun and several smaller armaments, together with an RDF cabin which housed 241 Radar equipment. The object of this Fort was to oversee the East Coast shipping lanes. After another short spell ashore, I think it was Portsmouth again, my naval experience up to this point in time had acted as a preface to my eventful year as a Radar rating/seaman aboard HMS Beagle, a 'B' class destroyer.

HMS Beagle was built by John Brown shipbuilders, ordered in March 1929, laid down in October of the same year, launched in late September, 1930 and completed on 9th.April 1931. It was a good looking warship and one that had experienced a colourful existence prior to my joining the crew.

During severe weather on 24th.October 1941 she had suffered a broken foremast and other damage, all of which had to be repaired in Greenock dockyard – at the same time she was fitted with Radar. HMS Beagle was to suffer more extensive damage in December 1941. Having proceeded to the Tyne for repairs, she was refitted, converted to a short-range escort and equipped with an early Hedgehog installation (anti U-boat devices), together with torpedo tubes, modified to fire a one ton depth charge. Before I joined 'Beagle', she had already sailed on escort duty for convoys PQ11, QP14, RA51, JW51A and JW52 to and from Northern Russia. Later on 'Beagle' was fitted with an improved Radar facility, ASW equipment and improved insulation ready for Arctic duties but, in true Admiralty fashion, was detached to Freetown, West Africa for local escort duties!

It was as an Able Seaman (Radar) that I became part of HMS Beagle's crew, my diary actually starting on 17th.June 1943. The Diary is the basis of this book but, where necessary, I have added further memories and additional information.

CHAPTER ONE

JOINING THE 'BEAGLE'

As I surveyed what was to be my second floating 'home of steel' HMS Beagle, certain things were obvious. 'Beagle' looked enormous compared with 'Sweet Briar' but certain things were similar such as the overall shape although, of course, 'Beagle' was much longer. The bridge structures were positioned forward, both had depth charge facilities aft, but differences were more obvious e.g. 'Beagle' had two funnels, one just behind the bridge and the other virtually amidships as opposed to the corvette's one, and she had two large calibre guns situated forward. Another thing that caught my eye was the Radar cabin, perched high on the bridge in an unimpeded position (for obvious reasons) which was to share my company for long periods of time over the coming year.

The general layout of the living quarters of both craft consisted of officers' wardroom aft and the ratings' mess decks forward with their associated 'heads' (toilets and showers) on the lower deck level. I noticed that the lower half of the crews' quarters was below the waterline, with a line of portholes each side able to be opened when required. The galley was situated on the upper deck just behind the bridge. Concentrating on the 'Beagle' the two large guns were virtually above us and in front of the bridge, and this meant that the ammunition was stored near to our quarters, not a happy arrangement! Vertical ladders connected the various levels, thus saving space.

Members of the crew were grouped according to their specialisms, with Radar ratings sharing accommodation with seaman, signallers etc., whilst stokers

HMS Beagle at speed. (IWM. A1877)

1

(responsible for the engine room) shared a separate mess deck nearer to their duties. The accommodation was basic of course, and members of the crew slept in hammocks which, during action stations remained slung and, although creating difficulty of movement around the mess, made for a quick response when required during the hours of darkness.

All modern warships use metal in their construction, for the hull, the decks, the bulwarks, the bridge etc., strong and serviceable, but uncompromising and with difficult surfaces in cold climes! I always felt that there was something aesthetically pleasing about the lines of destroyers like those of the 'Beagle', proportionally satisfying and built for speed and fighting power - there was nothing like the sight of a destroyer speeding at thirty knots through Neptune's playground.

As I boarded this modern man-o-war via the gangplank, my feelings were a mixture of anticipation and apprehension – what was the future about to reveal?

We left Pompey (Portsmouth Dockyard) at 9pm on Thursday 17th June and anchored in the solent. Earlier in the day in the early afternoon, a Liberty Boat had taken some of the crew, including myself, for what was to be a last trip ashore for some time. Shore leave lasted about five hours, during which time I brought some strawberries, had a haircut, and took some flowers to Mrs Wilson as a parting gift (I had made friends with the family during my time in Portsmouth). Finding her not at home, I gave the flowers to her daughter Pam.

CHAPTER TWO

PREPARATION FOR CONVOY DUTY

One of the things that servicemen had to get used to during wartime was unusual sleep patterns (getting to sleep and getting up at irregular times during the day and night). So it was not surprising for the 'Beagle' to join a convoy off the south coast at 4am on Friday 18th June, heading west. The crew's quarters being restricted for size, movement and comfort etc. for obvious reasons, it was important that individual members got on with each other and by and large this was the case. With our motley collection of human beings from all walks of life, mostly conscripted, co-operation was an important commodity.

My main job was to operate the Radar equipment and so I found myself 'on watch' (on duty) at 8pm (the 'first' watch) sailing at 7 knots, a situation which continued for the next two days, resulting in our arrival at Scapa Flow, Orkney Islands, a large naval base. This was on Monday 21st June and we anchored to a buoy at noon. Scapa Flow, as any sailor who has visited it will tell you, is one of the most godforsaken places on earth, with a large population of sheep and vast areas of desolation, at least it was then. There were warships at anchor as far as the eye could see, and this was to be our base for a few days. On Tuesday and Wednesday we were engaged in Sea Trials, broken up by the occasional game of Tombola (Bingo).

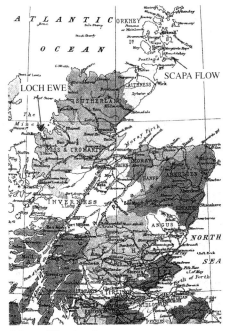

After Sea Trials on Thursday (24th June) I was able to go ashore from 4pm to 7pm and experience what little habitation existed, what there was mainly benefited the navy and I was able to enjoy the film, 'Kings Row'. My duties aboard HMS Beagle were two-fold, the most important being the operation of the Radar equipment and the other to include seamanship which, incidentally, involved rowing the whaler, a duty that had occupied me during the forenoon.

The following day, Friday, I went to the Dome Teacher for further practise as

Map of Scotland.

a Radar operator, engaging me until almost noon. Finding no Liberty Boat to return us to the 'Beagle' (she had left for further trials without notice) we realised that there must have been a sudden change of plan and that we were stranded! To kill time I went to the cinema again, after having dinner in the canteen, only to see 'Kings Row' for a second time! After the film I went to the depot ship HMS Tyne and saw another film, 'Random Harvest', starring Greer Garson and Ronald Colman, eventually returning to the 'Beagle' in our own motor boat, ready for a good night's sleep.

Another day- what excitement was in store? It was Saturday and at 8pm I rowed for half an hour. The Admiral came abroad at 11am, presumably to discuss with the Captain our 'training' progress and, not being involved(!), I went ashore in the early afternoon for about six hours. I endured yet another showing of 'Kings Row', followed by an ENSA play in the saloon bar.

'Beagle' proceeded out into the flow for small-arms practice just before midnight. It was a naval practice to hold a weekly Sunday service on board ship, depending on the prevailing situation, the ship's whereabouts, the weather etc. although the ritual was more likely to take place on larger ships, battleships, cruisers etc. On Sunday (27th.June) we held a forenoon Church Service and, as far as I can remember, it was compulsory for the crew as a whole. In the afternoon I went sailing in the whaler again, this time with 'Jimmy' (the First Lieutenant). The afternoon, being off-duty, was spent in sleeping, the day being rounded off with an evening bath (probably a shower).

An example of oiling at sea. The hose can be seen joining the ships. (IWM. A10693)

We practised oiling (refuelling) on Monday, not an easy operation, as this meant sailing alongside an oil tanker at the same speed and direction and at a specified distance, so that a heavy duty hose could be coupled to both ships enabling the oil to flow into the 'Beagle' tanks.

For reasons that I cannot recall, I received two days' 'elevens' (a form of punishment), the number presumably referring to a list, with punishments graded according to their severity. This was the only punishment that I received during the whole of my wartime career in the Navy!

An important event took place on 28th.June, important to me that is, in that I qualified for the rank of Leading Seaman, often called the 'hook' due to the sewing on of an anchor on the left sleeve. The day was rounded off by engaging in a night time small calibre shoot. Tuesday saw the start of my 'elevens' punishment – again I cannot remember what form it took (it cannot have been too drastic!). We took part in some more small calibre shooting trials and, during the evening, relaxed by enjoying a swim.

Trials continued on 30th.June and I was able to complete my 'elevens', with a sigh of relief, eventually tying up alongside HMS Tyne in the early evening, enabling me to attend an ENSA show aboard this large depot ship. There was also a performance of 'Arabian Nights'(?), the day ending with a bath (shower?). One might get the impression from reading these memoirs, based on my diary entries, that life was somewhat dull and monotonous, but this was not the case because of the effort needed for the myriad activities described, plus the need for 100% concentration. 'Trials' were continued on Thursday and Friday, at the conclusion of which we berthed alongside HMS Brilliant, another destroyer. There were no Trials on Saturday and we remained alongside 'Brilliant', spending the afternoon doing lots of dhobying and the evening playing Tombola.

We were about halfway through the Sea Trials based on Scapa Flow and the proficiency of the crew had improved significantly, but there was still some way to go. The secret of being an efficient Convoy Escort was quick response and team-work and these were the aims of this training.

During the forenoon of Sunday 4th.July we attended a Church Service, this to be the last one for some time, and I went ashore for the last time in the afternoon, partaking of two meals and playing snooker – not at the same time of course! I also saw yet another film entitled ' They've got me covered', with Bob Hope playing the lead. Monday seemed endless, with Trials from 0900 to 1500, followed by an evening of dhobying and ending with a relaxing bath. HMS Brilliant returned from her exercises in the 'flow' in the early hours of Tuesday - I was able to report this because my 'watch' was on duty and so I was awake! Tuesday saw more Trials outside the anchorage of Scapa Flow and in the main current, after which we berthed alongside a tanker at about teatime, moving to a depot ship to take on stores, and eventually reaching anchor at five o'clock.

Trials involving a torpedo shoot and a small arms shoot, in the company of HMS Renown (a battleship), started at 0700 on Wednesday 7th.July. 'Renown' looked resplendently menacing against the diminutive 'Beagle'. We were, nevertheless, an important part of the scheme of things, being a smaller target, very manoeuvrable and armed with a devastating weapon, the torpedo, 'Scharnhorst's' undoing in a few month's time! The Trials with 'Renown', together with HMS Sheffield and HMD Diamede continued on Thursday and involved Radar ratings (including me) using the RDF equipment to give range and direction for a two and a half hour 'shoot' which, fortunately, proved successful. We were glad to return to harbour on Friday 9th.July, with 'Renown', to enjoy(?) an afternoon of 'make and mend' (repairing clothes and darning socks etc.), but at 6.30pm we were out in the 'flow' again for the purpose of calibrating the HFDF(?), the latter part of the evening taking on a similar routine as many had before, dhobeying and bathing.

Readers will remember that earlier I had anticipated that the last shore leave that we enjoyed would be the final one before taking up convoy duty but I was wrong. Having anchored at a buoy at 7.30am, shore leave was granted from 1320 to 1845, a matter of nearly three and a half hours, during which time I had the opportunity to play the piano at the cinema. I do not think it was for a silent film! 'Beagle' left harbour at 7pm for two hours, for what reason I cannot recall and on Sunday we spent another eight hours at sea for more exercises. We took on ammunition at 5pm later that day and I was involved in this, it being one of my 'seamanship' duties. This lasted best part of an hour and was very hard work (no ammunition is light, especially shells for the large calibre guns) and I felt particularly 'chokka'! (fed up).

There was a 'buzz' (rumour) going round the ship's company that home leave was in the offing and that the Trials were complete. On Monday we 'worked ship' which meant cleaning the ship and attending to the various chores that needed to be done for the smooth running of HMS Beagle. I went for a trip in the Motor Boat to collect the R.A.D. (Rear Admiral?) who boarded us at 11am to bid the ship's company farewell, our Trials being successful, 'Beagle' being 'ready for action'.

After leaving HMS Brilliant alongside an oil-tanker, her ship's company probably feeling a little jealous of our impending return to England and 'leave', there remained one last exercise to be performed, that of oiling at sea with the cruiser HMS Shropshire, a tricky operation as I mentioned earlier. This was completed successfully. It was with some relief that at 3.15pm we sailed for Greenock, our base at present. The ship's company was divided into 'watches' so that some members of the crew were responsible for the safe running of 'Beagle' whilst the others rested. Starboard Watch was on duty during this trip from 2000 to 2400 (midnight) and that included yours truly.

We arrived at Greenock at 9am on Tuesday 13th. July, went alongside at 10.30am, and proceeded on leave at 11.45am. I reached Glasgow at 1.20pm where, if my memory serves me correctly, I had a haircut somewhere in the station complex. I caught the 5.40pm train and travelled all night, reaching London, Euston on Wednesday morning at 0600. The London 'Underground'(Tube) took me to Northfield Station and home. On this occasion the leave was a short one, just

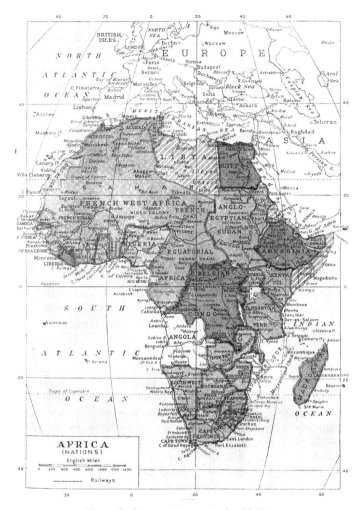

Map of Africa as it was in the 1940's.

Wednesday, Thursday, Friday and Saturday. The 10.55pm train from Euston took me north again to Greenock, and I arrived back on board 'Beagle' at 2pm, allowing me time to go to the cinema again to see a film at 7.30pm, 'Yank at Oxford'. Home leave had been very welcome after the hard work of the Trials, coupled with disjointed living schedules, broken sleep etc. As usual I had taken my tobacco and rum ration home to my father as I was a non-smoker. I was, however, to discover how essential it was to use the rum ration myself in the cold climes of the North Atlantic, and North Russia, where the 'Beagle' was to find itself in the not too distant future.

CHAPTER THREE

WEST AFRICA, HERE WE COME!

As I said in the introduction, 'Beagle' had been prepared for service with Russian Convoys but the Admiralty, in its wisdom(?), decided to send us for Convoy duty mainly off the west coast of Africa. With the Trials at Scapa Flow out of the way, we were ready to assume convoy duty and so, on Monday 19th.July 1943, we took on oil at 10am, leaving Greenock at 5pm and reaching Ireland at 10pm. There is no note in my diary but I presume we docked in Belfast harbour. I went around in the Motor Boat carrying out various duties, eventually returning to the 'Beagle' at 0030 for well-earned sleep. We left Ireland on Tuesday with a convoy of 16 ships, accompanied by 7 escorts including ourselves, sailing at a speed of 12 knots, an economical speed as far as fuel was concerned, but fast enough to make it difficult for U-boats to attack.

We were, I believe, transporting troops. I think my feelings, now that we were doing what we had been trained to do, were a mixture of excitement, anticipation and apprehension. My Duty Watch was the 'Morning Watch', 0400 to 0800 (breakfast time). I always felt that this was the second most difficult watch, the worst being the 'Middle Watch', midnight to 4am (0000 – 0400). It was a matter of keeping awake and alert so that early warning could be given, should the convoy be in danger. Staring at a small, green Radar screen for hours on end not only made the eyes tired, but made concentration difficult. I have described the workings of Radar equipment elsewhere. On Wednesday the weather was lovely with calm seas, sunshine and blue skies, in fact one could imagine being on a luxury cruise on a large passenger ship. This was except for the fact that it was war-time and conditions on a destroyer were far from luxurious, the food being basic, the accommodation cramped, added to the fact that submarines (U-boats) were always lurking ready to attack the convoy.

With a constant speed of 12 knots, the convoy was able to cover a fair distance each day – this speed had obviously been established by research and it was a common speed adopted by countless convoys. Thursday proved to be a dull day weather-wise but not in other respects because of the duties required of us. During the early hours of Friday 'Action Stations' were sounded (a klaxon), which meant that all of the crew members manned pre-arranged positions (guns, depth charges, extra lookouts, Radar equipment, central control etc.) and this happened twice more at 10am and 11am. Although nothing happened of any consequence, we did avoid a torpedo during the afternoon, confirming that there was a U-boat shadowing this motley collection of merchant ships. Otherwise, Friday was a quiet day with a repetition of the dull weather and we maintained our speed of 12 knots. Dull weather is to be preferred to sunshine when U-boats are lurking, although rough weather is even better. It was a lovely day on Saturday and we left the convoy at 5am to reach Casablanca on Sunday, where we oiled about teatime. Fruit was taken on board and we were able to partake of some of it and, after enjoying another lovely day, departed at 7.30pm. Monday saw a repeat of the fine weather and we rejoined the convoy at 7am. which, by this time consisted of 7 merchant ships and 3 escorts.

Tuesday 27th.1943 proved to be a momentous day in the progress of this World War, MUSSOLINI resigned! For us it was another gorgeous day, as was Wednesday and Thursday, the convoy now numbering 5 ships (another joined later) and on Friday three more merchantmen joined, but the weather dulled and it rained. Saturday was much like many of the recent days from a weather and speed point of view and we reached Freetown, West Africa on Sunday 1st. August 1943, our West African base for the next few months.

CHAPTER FOUR

WEST AFRICAN CONVOY DUTY

Freetown was to be our base for several months, with an uninviting harbour and little of interest ashore, and a depot ship HMS Philoctetees virtually permanently anchored in the harbour and very necessary for replenishing our stores and providing a modicum of entertainment. On arrival at this naval base at 4pm we tied up alongside an oil tanker where we remained for the night. The following day we proceeded to the water tanker and subsequently to anchor. It was somewhat ironic taking on water because it started to rain heavily, prompting us to walk about in our bathing costumes! Not a pretty sight! Incidentally, when it rains in that part of the world, it really buckets down.

A group of us went ashore in the early afternoon and unwisely drank some of the local brew, sometimes called 'Jungle Juice'. I vaguely remember a ramshackle hut where we consumed this mind-blowing concoction and how one of the other members of our group moved a seat that I was about to sit on, causing me sit on the floor. In the normal course of events it would have caused a titter but, in the inebriated state that we were in, it resulted in us all being helplessly overcome by concerted, uncontrollable laughter!! Eventually, having regained our composure, we returned to the 'Beagle' but, on reaching a wide stream, we were confronted with stepping stones that looked somewhat dangerous (I think we were still recovering from our previous experience!). We had been accompanied back to our ship by a small group of young natives begging for money and when they saw our predicament they offered to carry us across. Imagine the ludicrous picture of somewhat large matelots being transported across the water on the shoulders of these local inhabitants. After negotiating the stream, they followed us all the way back to the 'Beagle' presumably expecting some recompense which, in fact, I do not think was forthcoming. We had been warned about becoming involved with the local inhabitants for various reasons and I don't think we would have accepted help if we had been thinking clearly! We were rather relieved to get back on board, not being sure how aggressively the lads would back up their demands? We had bought some bananas whilst ashore.

During the afternoon of Tuesday (2nd.August) we engaged in the unattractive occupation of washing the ship's side – it was felt necessary to keep the ship clean, although I often wondered why, as the unwashed hull would surely have added to the camouflage? We went ashore again at 1.30pm and walked about the town, such that it was, eating bananas and monkey nuts. We also bought cigarettes cheaply (I bought a shoehorn?), refreshing ourselves with iced, lemon tea. Wednesday saw us painting ship during the forenoon, afternoon and evening until 6.30pm - slave labour! After supper we carried bread forward to the galley, the stores being aft (near the stern), hoisted the Motor Boat and, as I was no longer needed for any duties, I had a bath, ending the day with beloved (?) dhobying, eventually turning in at midnight. During the day I had traded something in for a pair of slippers, but I cannot remember what it was or why! I wrote an Airmail home, one of very few - I was not an enthusiastic correspondent.

At 6am on Thursday 5th.August we proceeded to the oiler to take on fuel and then to the water tanker, finally putting to sea at 10.30am. Instructions were given that no dhobying was to be done whilst we were at sea, not uncommon, in order to avoid a water shortage. We 'messed about' washing down the forecastle (forward part of the ship) and, after a rather dull morning with some rain and a lovely afternoon we joined a convoy of nine merchantmen – some had been in the previous convoy.

The convoy was engaged in troop transportation and was protected by six escorts and, as before, we adopted a speed of 12 knots. It may seem a contradiction in terms in recording the activity of the washing down of the forecastle whilst having made a reference to the limited supply of fresh water, but for all activities other than eating and bathing, sea water would have been used. Friday and Saturday were repeats of the previous days as far as weather and speed were concerned but, during the 'Dog Watch' on Saturday, I listened to records being played – I cannot recall the music titles, the equipment or the venue!

On Sunday 8th.August 1943 we left the convoy in the company of two merchantmen and, after taking them to Takoradi, we proceeded to Lagos accompanied by HMS Douglas, another destroyer. I wrote one of my infrequent letters home followed by some dhobying, my favourite activity (?) and this included seven pairs of shorts and a white front (somewhat like a present-day 'T' shirt).

Peter Ward in tropical clothes (2nd. from the left). Jock Miller (far right).

I ought to have mentioned earlier that, before embarking on West African Convoy Duty, the ship's company was issued with appropriate clothing, commonly referred to as 'Tropical Gear', for the hot climes. This consisted of mostly white cotton material and included shorts rather than bell-bottoms. We reached Lagos at 7am on Monday and, with 'Douglas', went alongside an oiler. HMS Bulldog, another destroyer similar to 'Beagle', joined us three hours later and we left harbour with two merchantmen, rejoining the original convoy in the early afternoon, which now consisted of eleven merchantmen and six escorts. There was a heavy swell (long, undulating waves).

Things do not always go to plan, not even with the Senior Service and, as we left Lagos, we nearly collided with an oil tanker, having nearly taken away the anchor chain which runs through outlets on the forecastle. Some of us were doing seaman's duties on the forward part of 'Beagle' and did we move! There could have been a serious accident. I was on First Watch (8pm - midnight) and spotted an echo on the RDF (Radio Direction Finding) screen. It indicated something on the surface astern of us and we had to investigate, only to find that it was HMS Douglas!

The best way to describe the way that RADAR operated is as follows: an electric signal is sent by the transmitter, the signal being reflected on reaching an object in its path on the sea surface (much like a sound echo), subsequently returning to the initiating equipment and registering as a 'blip' on a screen (much like a present-day television screen) calibrated to show the distance of the reflecting object from the 'Beagle'. There was a communicating tube from the RDF Cabin to the Bridge, by means of which the RDF operator could inform the officer on watch, who would take the necessary action. The size of the 'blip' could also indicate to some extent the size of the object, most likely to be another ship or a U-boat etc. We were joined by a couple more escorts and, being another lovely day (as was the following day) we continued at the commonly adopted speed of 12 knots.

On Thursday at 11am we left the convoy with Douglas and Wolverine and three quarters of an hour later were sailing up the River Congo where, after oiling, we anchored at the river mouth to keep 'watch'. Incidentally, the mess deck (our living quarters in the forward part of the ship and partly below deck) was chaotic, with water swilling around at a depth of three feet! This was due to the fact that, prior to reaching the River Congo, we had turned at speed whilst chasing what was thought to be a U-boat.

As 'Beagle' heeled over, something which happens to most sea craft that turn either to port or starboard at speed, it allowed vast quantities of water to flood through the open portholes as we had no time to close them, no warning having been given before the sudden turn. Quick decisions had to be made throughout the war, sometimes with unfortunate and surprising results. With everything swimming around it took some time to restore order and even longer for things to dry out. RDF and SD (I think that this was similar to Radar but to detect underwater objects – Asdics?).

CHAPTER FIVE

'NEPTUNE REX' PAYS A CALL

The battleship HMS Revenge lay outside the mouth of the River Congo and on Friday we left the river to patrol around this enormous and powerful warship to protect it from possible ' U-boat attack. We patrolled around 'Revenge' all day and all night, in fact five destroyers patrolled whilst she took on oil. She was, of course, too big to enter the river. We were still going round in circles on Monday! At midday HMS Resolution, another battleship, was also involved in oiling and there were two merchantmen near the 'Battlers'.

I remarked earlier about the erratic hours that befell us, although this was probably true of all soldiers and airmen too and, having slept from 10pm until midnight, I took up my duties for the Middle Watch. Later, after three attempts, we managed to tie up alongside the oil tanker - it was the case of third time lucky! At 7am we cast off and proceeded to sea. At 8am I took up my duties for the Forenoon Watch (which ended at midday) after which I was able to catch up on some sleep until 6.30pm that is, after snatching some lunch. My next duty was First Watch and what a nightmare Watch it was because, throughout the night, we were in the extremely strong River Congo current, so strong that it broke four wires (hawsers that secure a ship to another vessel or the quayside etc.). We eventually left the Congo with two merchantmen, plus 'Revenge', 'Resolution' and four destroyers. Monday, 16th.August was a fairly good day weatherwise and we maintained the usual speed, the crew awaiting the ritual which befell every ship in these latitudes.

At 7.45pm precisely, Father Neptune (a member of the ship's company dressed up of course – it was thought to be Miller) boarded (!) HMS Beagle and made a speech, with the ship's company gathered on the forecastle. At 10am the following day we had the 'Crossing the Line' ceremony, which consisted of several of those gathered submitting themselves to be lathered around the chin (rather liberally!) with soapsuds, followed by being shaved with a giant wooden razor! It was not long after the ship's crew regained some sort of sanity that 'Action Stations' was sounded but proved to be a false alarm – whale echoes on the Asdics perhaps? Because of the lack of fresh water (again!) no dhobying was allowed. Wednesday saw us continuing on our way, the weather being congenial with, counting 'Beagle', six escorts, 2 battleships and 2 merchantmen. The lovely weather remained with us through Thursday and Friday, a speed of 12 knots being maintained in spite of sub scares. Four merchantmen passed us proceeding in the opposite direction without, it would seem, any escort vessels. I was on duty during the First Watch on Friday, with Saturday proving to be another uneventful day except for more 'sub' scares and, maintaining our usual speed, we reached Freetown at 9am, where we oiled before anchoring.

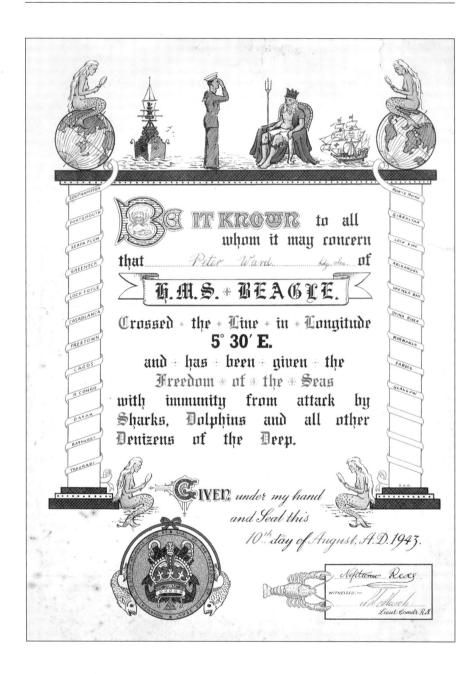

'*Crossing the Line*' *certificate*.

The weather was conducive to sleeping on the upper deck until, unfortunately, it started to rain at 2 o'clock in the morning, forcing us to go below and thus bringing to an end our enjoyment of the cool night air. It rained on and off and we were able to collect the rainwater in buckets, thus augmenting our fresh water supply. This situation continued throughout Sunday and Monday but, with the rain becoming more spasmodic, we were able to wash the ship's side - what joy?

With the rain being intermittent on Tuesday, we were able to scrub one of the funnels, making it possible to paint it silver the following day. We were able to go ashore for five or so hours during the afternoon and early evening, spending the time swimming (I forget where) and walking around the town enjoying the lovely weather - if only it hadn't been wartime. We bought a pumpkin, bananas, a mango and a pomegranate, and it was only then I realised what proportion of a pomegranate was made up of pips! During the afternoon of Thursday we went shore-wards again in spite of the rain, but this time to order sanitary blocks (disinfectant) for the 'heads' (naval toilets).

I must confess that the thought had crossed my mind as to the wisdom of painting the funnel silver, thinking that surely we would be more easily spotted with the reflected light etc. But on the afternoon of Friday 27th August we painted it with its planned colour, silver being an undercoat! After the painting we were allowed ashore again, thank goodness. Our Watch was on duty on the Saturday and during the day we received mail, quite amazing considering that we were in Freetown, West Africa in wartime, a considerable distance from home!! I spent the forenoon of Sunday in the Motor Boat but was able to take more shore leave in the afternoon, buying more bananas and a pomegranate which, in spite of the pips, was very pleasant to eat. The ship's company was issued with four oranges each - big deal!

Early on Monday morning, after oiling, we left Freetown to go in search of a Spanish merchantman (Monte-ah?), reputed to be carrying contraband and our speed on this occasion was 25 knots! There is nothing like a destroyer, a man-o-war, carving its way through a calm, flat sea, its sleek shape matching its movement through the water and, with its armaments looking strong and aggressive, ready for anything

Destroyers travelling at speed.
(IWM. A10296)

that the enemy could throw at her and equally ready to attack when necessary. We never found the Spanish ship, but we passed a Portuguese steamer sailing we knew not where but that being all, we reduced speed to the normal 12 knots to resume patrol. HMS Corfu was due to join us as 'back up' and, whilst we were patrolling on Wednesday (in more lovely weather) she caught up with us and subsequently passed to us eight, very welcome, sacks of bread. Thursday was similar, but at 0545 (5.45am) on Friday, 3rd September 1943 the unthinkable happened, the RDF (Radar) equipment broke down! This equipment was the 'eyes' of the 'Beagle', especially during the hours of darkness, and the electrical engineer got to work 'at the double'.

At breakfast time we reached Dakar, resuming patrol after spending seven hours there. This situation continued on Saturday until we reached Bathurst at 2pm on Sunday, where we went alongside the jetty to take on oil (a messy operation!) and to anchor at 8pm. During this period at Bathurst and whilst I was ashore, I gave my watch to an African to repair. I must have been very naïve. We worked ship (engaged in activities to keep the ship in good repair) during the forenoon of Monday and then I went ashore via the Motor Boat for four or so hours in the afternoon. During this time I swam for about two hours before starting to chase up the watch that I had inadvisably parted with earlier. I eventually retrieved it at the 'eleventh' hour, just managing to catch the Liberty Boat back to the 'Beagle'.

We left Bathurst at 9am the following day to rejoin a convoy, this time travelling at 10 knots and accompanied by 3 escorts and 2 'troopers' (troop-carrying merchantmen). Our diet was pretty basic at the best of times and the Captain, in his wisdom, ordered Depth Charges to be dropped (these are barrel-like containers filled with explosive which can be set to explode at a variety of depths and are mostly used to sink U-boats - they are released on runners over the stern) with the express object of trying to catch some fish!!! The idea was to stun the fish and catch them when they floated to the surface. Suffice to say that the experiment was not terribly successful! I do not know how the Captain's Log Book justified the use of Depth Charges for this purpose, but assume it showed that we were attempting to sink a U-boat at the time!?

On Wednesday we took on board an HM Inspector of Prisons, for what reason I cannot recall, nor do I know from whence he came. He gave a talk on 'Radio Beagle' presumably on the topic of prisons, but this was not recorded in the Diary. Because of the climate of this part of the world in which we were operating, there was always the possibility of sleeping on deck in the open air (mentioned earlier) but this was often impossible because of heavy rain. It was disappointing when we were not able to experience floating through the night on a millpond-like sea, sleeping in the fresh air. I ought to mention that there were members of the crew on watch day and night, the U-boat menace never being far away. I remember thinking that I would be better off on deck rather that cocooned in the bowels of the ship in the event of being torpedoed!

0800 (8am) on Thursday saw our arrival in Freetown again and we oiled ship and anchored, after which and in spite of the rain, we worked throughout the forenoon. Our 'Watch' was on duty but we managed to buy some bananas, presumably from one of the natives in small African boats that plied their wares around the harbour. Another 'big deal' worthy of mention – we were issued with two oranges!! Friday saw us working ship in the morning and ashore in the afternoon, where we enjoyed a swim in a fresh water pool. The RDF equipment had been repaired and was now working thank goodness, the 'Beagle' being at a distinct disadvantage with loss of one of its 'eyes'. We worked ship during Saturday forenoon and it was on this day that I put in a request to take a Petty Officer course, my request being granted. I went aboard the depot ship Philoctetes with some watches but cannot remember the reason or where I obtained them! Another period of rainfall greeted us on Sunday and I was in the Motor Boat for eight and a half hours non-stop, starting at 1pm. This was quite demanding and there were no Trades Unions to argue otherwise! For some reason the whaler, a craft that served several purposes including being used as a lifeboat, went adrift and we had to search for it. When the whaler was found we were relieved that it had come to no harm. We weighed anchor at 7.30am on Monday to do a 'shoot', similar to those that we had experienced at Scapa Flow whilst in training, this to involve all our armaments, the control centre, Radar etc. Warships included were the destroyers 'Boadicea', 'Wolverine' and a sloop, not forgetting the destroyer 'Bulldog', the same class as 'Beagle'. At 5pm, after a long day's activity and feeling exhausted, we anchored in Freetown harbour and, for my sins, our Watch was on duty.

On Tuesday 13th.September we left Freetown to join a convoy of six merchantmen, four destroyers and a sloop, this time with a speed of 13 knots. We had five passengers aboard, an RAF airman and 2 Naval personnel, together with 2 RNVR Officers. RNVR is short for Royal Navy Volunteer Reserve, personnel who were involved with the Navy in peace time and who would have been 'called up' as soon as war broke out. We continued on our way on Wednesday at the same speed, it being a fine day and, surprise, surprise, all my dhobying was up to date! Being in a very hot climate and wearing white cotton clothing, it was none too easy to keep things clean and smart. On Thursday for some reason, the convoy speed increased to 14 knots and, to the embarrassment of all, the RDF equipment broke down again. We reached Takoradi at 8am and tied up alongside the jetty – we were Duty Watch. During Friday morning we washed the ship's side, a delightful job!

I managed to get lost in the afternoon whilst ashore, an uncomfortable situation to find oneself in amongst the ramshackle huts of this African settlement, the people being somewhat unpredictable and me with not a word of their language? I eventually discovered my whereabouts and managed to purchase another watch (Seconda?), ending the day with a visit to the cinema to see a film, the title of which remains a mystery. The forenoon of Saturday saw us painting the ship's side that had been prepared the day before, an equally delightful occupation, followed by shore leave in the afternoon. On Sunday we completed painting the ship's side, went ashore in the afternoon and, after attending a 7.15pm service, brought the day to a close with some 'eats' (food). I thought we had completed the painting, but I was wrong and, after another morning of drudgery, I was able to leave 'Beagle' again, this time to visit an RAF Camp where a film was showing entitled 'Cargo of Innocents', and this nicely rounded off the day. The next day, Tuesday, was another one of those boring ones, with more painting, Duty Watch and dhobying in the afternoon.

The next couple of days were a little complicated for us as far as ship movement was concerned, with 'Beagle' leaving Takoradi jetty at 8.15am on Wednesday, 22nd.September and anchoring for a couple of hours before proceeding to Lagos with two merchantmen and three destroyers including us. We reached Lagos at 8am on Thursday, leaving the merchantmen to continue into Lagos harbour, whilst we returned to Takoradi, arriving there early morning on Friday. After anchoring for a short time we left, this time with two merchantmen, a corvette and two destroyers (Be.Wo.) but one of the merchantmen developed engine trouble, delaying us for half an hour.

This was to be an important day for me (Friday, 24th.September 1943) because I was confirmed as Coxswain of the Motor Boat. The Motor Boat was an important link between ship and shore, and was continually in use for one thing and another. On Saturday we arrived at Lagos in the early afternoon, oiled and tied up alongside the 'Empire Flamingo'. At 7.30pm shore leave was granted and we proceeded ashore dressed in 'duck suits' i.e. hot weather clothing issue of a white, cotton, short-sleeve top, white shorts, white socks and white shoes. It was dark and, after a short walk I found the Palace Hotel where I had dinner, returning on board at 10pm. On Sunday it rained for most of the morning and I officially took over as Motor Boat Coxswain at 12.30pm. Fortunately the afternoon was fairly easy and enjoyable and so, after tying up at a buoy, I turned in at 1am on the morning of Monday. I mentioned earlier about the 'unsocial' hours! I was responsible for the M.B. during Monday morning and went ashore in a 'bum' boat in the afternoon (I cannot remember the origin of the word 'bum', but it was a craft that carried us to land and back) visiting the King George V café for a meal. We went back on board at 7pm and after an hour proceeded ashore again to see the film 'Pride and Prejudice', starring Greer Garson and Laurence Olivier. On Tuesday I went ashore during the afternoon to get more 'sanitary blocks' for our toilets, on the instructions of Jimmy (First Lieutenant, answerable to the Captain) – these were most important for the hygiene of the ship – and managed to do some shopping myself. I took over the Motor Boat on Wednesday at 12.30pm, spending a busy time for several hours with only ten minutes out of the boat (!), which included taking 'Beagle's' officers some distance down the river during the afternoon to bathe – the forenoon had been busy too. Later in the afternoon we went ashore for more shopping and I could not resist a return visit to the King George V café for more lovely food, after which we went back aboard, the day ending with supper and bed.

During the morning of Thursday, the last day of September, I went ashore again for 'Jimmy', this time taking an anchor (?) to the Yacht Club. I tried to obtain cash from my Post Office savings book but for some reason was unsuccessful and later tried to sell a watch – I seemed to have a thing about watches! I returned aboard in the early afternoon and managed to borrow ten shillings, a lot of money in those days, from Gunner 'T'. Taking over as Motor Boat coxswain, I made half a dozen trips before the M.B. was hoisted aboard at 3.30pm. Another memory, not recorded in my Diary, but one which still remains fairly vivid, was an occasion whilst we were tied up in Lagos harbour. There were traders along the water front sitting cross legged with their wares in front of them; incidentally I bought a couple of African hard wood busts made for book ends, which I still own. As I watched, two sailors (not from the 'Beagle' I hasten to add!) approached one of the traders and crouched, legs apart and, holding one of the objects for sale, started haggling with the trader over the price, the accepted way of buying things. Suddenly, to my amazement the sailor, supposedly buying whatever it was that he was holding in one hand, used his other hand to pass other objects for sale between his legs, the other sailor who was close behind him depositing them in a bag. After a short time, the haggling sailor obviously feeling they were pushing their luck, handed back the object used for the haggling and both sailors moved away quickly with their spoils, the trader seemingly unaware that anything untoward had happened. It all happened so quickly and appeared amusing at the time, but in retrospect one's conscience should have dictated some action!

We left our mooring half an hour later, this time with a convoy of six merchantmen, escorted by the destroyers 'Bulldog, Douglas, Wolverine' and, of course, ourselves, destination Pointe Noire. The convoy enjoyed lovely weather during Friday and Saturday, and we arrived at Pointe Noire at 5pm, only to leave again two and a half hours later to patrol outside the harbour for the whole of the night. ASDICS (equipment similar to RADAR but for use under water) was used to spot marauding U-boats. At the crack of dawn on Monday, 3rd.October we left Pointe Noire with another convoy, the escorts consisting of a French Battleship 'Lorraine' and destroyers 'Wolverine, Bulldog, Boadicea and Bea—(?)' , not forgetting a 'Trooper', with a daytime speed of 13 knots, increasing to 16 knots at night. Tuesday and Wednesday saw more good weather, with 'Wolverine' and 'Boadicea' leaving during the afternoon for other duties or to refuel and returning at10pm. 'Douglas' had left earlier at 10.30am, 'Boadicea' leaving early afternoon. We oiled at Takoradi and on Thursday, 7th.October the convoy proceeded, 'Douglas' rejoining at 11pm. There were 'buzzes'(rumours) going the rounds of 'Beagle' that our West African duties were coming to an end and that we were to return to the UK! Little did we know how great the contrast would be between our tropical spell and what was to come! The pleasant faces of the climate, weather, sea etc. of West Africa were due to change dramatically! Friday saw another balmy day, with the convoy proceeding uneventfully.

We reached Freetown at 5pm., probably for the last time and, after oiling, tied up alongside the 'Strathmore', where we received mail. The weather, continuing to be very pleasant, produced a lovely sunset. There was a boom protecting the harbour and we sailed just outside it on Sunday for an HFDF call, returning just after midday. It was my turn to be Duty Coxswain and, after a busy session, I snatched some well-needed sleep. There are two items in the diary referring to 'Mid. in the boat' which I do not understand, but can only suggest that a Midshipman (officer) was in the Motor Boat for some reason. Hands (members of the crew) were engaged in washing the ship's side yet again. Monday, 11th.October found me as Duty Coxswain during the morning, but I managed to 'get my head down'(went to sleep) in the afternoon, spending the evening writing letters.

Freetown - buying bananas.

The weather encouraged the taking of photographs. On Tuesday I just messed about in the morning, officiating as M.B. Coxswain after lunch for another busy period during which I had to wait for the Captain, Lieutenant Commander Murch, who was aboard HMS Malcolm. Arriving back at the 'Beagle', it must have been at least midnight, the Captain must have felt sorry for us and gave each of us a tot of whisky, a rare occurrence, and we eventually turned in at 1.30am. on Wednesday! In spite of lack of sleep, Wednesday was another duty day as M.B. Coxswain and, with the mess deck (living quarters) being painted during the forenoon, we had to eat our midday meal on the upper deck.

'There were more strong 'buzzes' about going back home and I went ashore in the afternoon and bought a stalk of bananas, quite a large stalk with many bananas. As far as I can remember it had to be stored with the ammunition. Just imagine firing bananas at the enemy - perhaps they would have slipped up!!

Descriptions of places visited in West Africa

Contemporary background information of the places visited by HMS Beagle during its tour of duty as an escort destroyer based at Sierra Leone, West Africa. The descriptions of the places, mainly ports, are as they were during the 1940's, at the time of the writing of the Diary.

ACCRA: A seaport and, since 1876, capital of the British Gold Coast colony and situated 8 miles east of the Cape Coast. It had a railway communication with

Takoradi harbour, the line running 365 miles via Kumasi in Ashanti. A municipality, Accra was an air, telegraph and wireless station and had a lighthouse, banks, an Anglican Church and a race course. There was no harbour, landing being by surf-boat. Exports consisted of cocoa, gold dust, palm oil, ivory, rubber, gum and timber. Population approximately 70,000.

BATHURST: A seaport of West Africa. The capital of the British colony of Gambia, it was situated on St. Mary's Island, a sandbank about ¾ mile long and 1¼ miles broad, and was 7 miles from the mouth of the River Gambia. The island was largely a swamp, but the town was clean and well regulated, trading in rice, cotton, tobacco, fruit, rubber, hides, gum and wax. It had cable communication with Sierra Leone and St. Vincent (Cape Verde). Population approximately 6,000.

CASABLANCA: A seaport of French Morocco and situated on the Atlantic coast between Mazagan and Rabat, it had a maritime trade. In 1938 the port handled 4,000,000 tons of shipping. It was connected by railway with Mazagan, Marrakesh, Rabat and Fez. It had a wireless station and a cable terminus. The town was founded by the Portuguese on the site of a settlement destroyed in 1465, and was occupied by the French in 1907, after the murder of French workmen at the harbour.
    (The Casablanca area was an important meeting place of the Allies during the Second World War). Population approximately 453000. (131,000 were European).

DAKAR: A seaport of Senegal and the administrative capital of French West Africa. It stood on the Cape Verde peninsula, the most westerly point of Africa, and afforded a harbour for the largest ships. It was connected by railway with St. Louis, was a coaling station, and the terminus of the French cable from Brest. Dakar was founded as a dependency of Goree in 1862. The administration was transferred to it from St. Louis in 1903. The circumscription of Dakar and dependencies ranked as a French colony, having its own governor, bishopric and budget. Population approx. 182,000.

FREETOWN: (The base for HMS Beagle during its West African escort duties). A seaport and capital of Sierra Leone, British West Africa. The town was situated on the Sierra Leone River, with wooded mountains to the south and east and at the north west extremity of the Sierra Leone peninsula. European residences were on the highlands, reached by a mountain railway. Freetown was founded at Granville Town in 1788 as a home for West African slaves. The harbour was the finest and most important in West Africa. A railway ran inland to Pendembu, a distance of 228 miles. Motor roads were constructed, and there was connection by air with Great Britain. The chief exports were iron ore, palm kernels and oil, Kola nuts, cocoa, diamonds, ginger and hides. (Freetown was a Naval and RAF station during the Second World War and a terminal of its aeroplane ferry across Africa). Population approx. 55,000.

LAGOS: An island city in the western province of Nigeria. The city was the principal seaport of the colony and the seat of its central government. It was bombarded and captured by the British in 1851 and incorporated in the British Empire ten years later.

(When, after the entry of the Japanese into the Second World War and the seaways of the Indian Ocean were threatened, Lagos became of prime importance, its port forming a terminus of the transcontinental motor road and its aerodrome a vital link in airways to Cairo and the East). A railway connected Iddo on the mainland (which was joined by bridge to Lagos) with Kano in the north of Nigeria, crossing the River Niger at Jebba. Population approximately 175,000.

TAKORADI: A harbour of the Gold Coast, it was 3 miles west of Secondi and had railway communication with the interior and with Accra. Planned in 1921, it was opened in 1928 as the only harbour of consequence on the coast of Africa between Dakar and Pointe Noire. It had breakwaters, wharves and equipment to handle 5,000 tons of cargo, worth £4,000,000 a day. (When the Mediterranean route to Egypt was closed to Allied shipping during the Second World War, Takoradi became a supply base for the Allied armies in Egypt and North Africa; aircraft in crates were brought there by sea, assembled at an RAF maintenance unit and flown across Africa to Cairo.

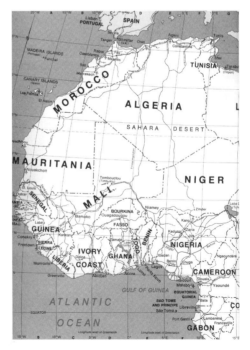

Map of North West Africa.

CHAPTER SIX

GOODBYE WEST AFRICA

The Motor Boat was hoisted at 2am on Thursday, 14th.October 1943, and we left for the UK at 6am, having taken passengers on board, RAF personnel etc. There was great excitement as we left Freetown with a convoy made of seven merchantmen, four destroyers, 'Bulldog, Douglas, Mal—(?) and Beagle' with whom we had joined forces at about midday, heading for Gibraltar. There must have been mixed feelings about leaving West Africa, with many pleasant memories as well as others. It was a perfect day and we maintained a speed of 13 knots, with the Captain addressing the Ship's Company at one point, confirming our programme as far as returning to England was concerned. The convoy reached Dakar at 2.30am.on Friday, another beautiful day, with the express purpose of taking on oil, leaving at 0530 on Saturday, again with clement weather. We sang hymns over the SRE (broadcasting equipment) at 7pm on this day, Sunday, 17th.October 1943, and we were greeted on Monday by another sunny day – I don't think they were connected (!) – but the weather was getting cooler as we went north. Tuesday and Wednesday were without incident.

We reached Gibraltar at noon on Friday, berthing at the Mole with the 'Bulldog, Boadicea and Duncan'. I was off duty throughout the morning, but took on my duties as M.B. Coxswain for the afternoon and evening. It fell to my lot to be Duty Coxswain on Saturday morning, but in the afternoon I had the unusual task of taking shorthand notes on a case for CERA, spending until 4pm. transcribing them! It had been some considerable time since I had used my shorthand skills and, once able to do one hundred words per minute, it made me realise how rusty I was. I was able to get ashore and walk to the Spanish border, after which I went to the 'pictures'. I had no duties on Sunday morning and I attended Divisions (Naval Church Service), after which I went ashore to draw money from my Post Office Savings Book, this time being more successful than the last! I was Duty Coxswain in the afternoon. Monday activities were similar to those of Sunday, with Motor Boat duties and note taking for the CERA case, again finding the transcribing rusty, and on this occasion it took until 5pm.after which I took a bath and relaxed. I was off-duty on Tuesday morning but duty Coxswain after lunch, during which time I 'crawled' round the harbour there being no lights, it being war-time, dropping off and picking up 'liberty men', the crew of the 'Beagle'. In the dark I had to avoid buoys and booms strewn around the harbour.

The Diary contains the word 'Aldis' on its own, and I presume this was to record that signalling (communicating with other ships etc.) was done by Aldis Lamp. This was a powerful lamp with which one could send Morse Code messages by a system of flashes, thus avoiding sending radio signals, which could have been picked up by the enemy. Wednesday saw minor excitement when, after I had completed my duty as Coxswain in the morning and was about to go ashore in the afternoon, the ship's company who were ashore were recalled at 4.30pm. so that we could proceed to sea at 7.45pm. on submarine (U-boat) patrol. In the event we returned to harbour having found nothing, but no chances could be taken.

CHAPTER SEVEN

THE TRANSITION – OUT OF THE FRYING PAN INTO THE FREEZER!

Having spent five months patrolling off the West Coast of Africa, 'Beagle's' duties in this area of World War II came to an end. We departed from Gibraltar at 11am on Friday, 29th.October 1943 with a convoy of six merchant ships and 3 escorts and headed for the Mediterranean to meet another convoy at 6pm. Turning around, we proceeded back through the Straits of Gibraltar at a speed of 15 knots but now with an enlarged convoy of twenty-four ships and eleven escorts, to head for the UK.

The weather was lovely on Saturday but getting cooler, with a choppy sea and a swell, with the ship's crew glad to be heading for 'Blighty' at last. Sunday and Monday proved to be similar, except for the fact that on Monday there were some submarine scares! On Tuesday the convoy proceeded on its way, but suffering from more 'sub' scares, only this time accompanied by enemy aircraft flying in the vicinity. Two of the escort frigates hunted for the U-boats and dropped depth charges, but had no luck in finding any marauding sub-mariners. Wednesday was another fine day and on Thursday, 4th.November we reached Ireland. Having oiled, we left at 1pm reaching Greenock at 5pm.

From Friday, 5th.November until Thursday, 11th.November we remained tied up alongside, either at Greenock or Gourock. We went home on leave on the 12th. November travelling from Gourock as far as I can recollect, enjoying home comforts, good food, a real bed and a good soak in a real bath, until Saturday, 20th. November when, without delay, we left Gourock at 11am to oil, leaving the Clyde at 3pm for Loch Ewe. Reaching Loch Ewe at 11am on Sunday, we lowered the Motor Boat for the usual ferrying duties – one of the M.B. crew, the bowman, fell in the 'drink'(sea), much to the amusement of the rest of the crew.

I have often wondered whether we knew what our next duties would involve when we left Freetown, i.e. Russian Convoys. Due to wartime demands of secrecy I rather think not and suspect that our first realisation of what was in store was the first Russian Convoy.

CHAPTER EIGHT

RUSSIAN CONVOYS

Thus starts the second half of the 'Beagle' Diary, albeit extending over seven months and including Russian Convoys and the 'D' Day landings. We left Loch Ewe on Monday at 10am. with a convoy of seventeen ships and five escorts, to experience lousy weather and very rough seas, a complete contrast to the West African patrols.

This was *Convoy JW54B (see Appendix A)*, the first Russian Convoy that HMS Beagle was to be involved with during the time that I was a member of the crew. It would be useful at this stage to say a word or two about the way convoys were organised, something that was not necessary during our duties over the last few months because the convoys were much smaller and the danger from U-boats less likely. All convoys proceeded in a standard formation with standard nomenclature.

THE AREA FOR ARCTIC OPERATIONS 1941-1945

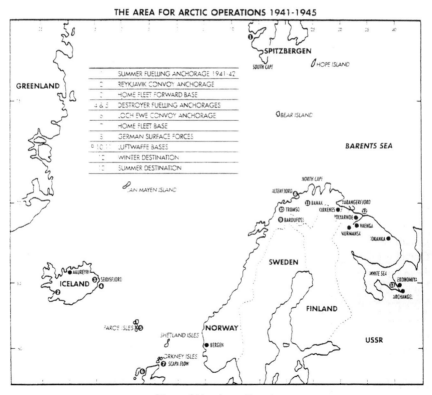

Map of Northern Russia.

The form of the convoy was a 'broad front' of a number of short columns, the norm being between 7 and 12 columns with three or four ships per column. Obviously, the larger the convoy the greater number of columns and ships therein, the record being the North Atlantic convoy HX 300 with 167 ships, 19 columns and up to 11 ships in some of them. Columns were consistently numbered in the same way for obvious reasons.

We continued through Tuesday and Wednesday with equally lousy weather, which did not improve on Thursday and, to make matters worse, we had to exist on two slices of bread per person per day, with very little hot water! I am sure that there was other food such as soup to keep body and soul together, but the bread remains in my memory. On Friday, with no improvement in the weather, eight destroyers joined the convoy and on Saturday, fortunately, the weather became fairly fine and calm. When I say fortunately, there were drawbacks to the better weather insofar that it made U-boat attacks more likely, submarines having better visibility and a steadier, torpedo firing possibility.

The better weather stayed with us during Sunday and made it possible to take on oil. This involved 'Beagle' picking up a large-bore pipe from the accompanying tanker, through which the oil would pass to our storage tanks. The oil would feed the ship's engines, supply fuel for equipment that produced electricity, heat, salt water purification, in fact all those things that kept 'Beagle' ready for action and maintained adequate living facilities. During refuelling, both vessels had to steer an identical course, maintain a consistent speed and distance, very difficult even in calm seas! This operation had to be completed as soon as possible because it made both vessels more vulnerable to attack, both having their manoeuvrable abilities lessened. The length of daylight was now reduced to four hours (10am to 2pm approx) and would continue to be so as we travelled north. Although the weather remained reasonably fine, we experienced snowstorms, which continued into Monday and Tuesday. On Wednesday we continued to enjoy fine weather and eight destroyers and ten merchantmen left the convoy for Murmansk and, with the snow still falling, it made visibility difficult.

When visibility is reduced RADAR comes into its own because the elements, generally speaking, do not reduce its ability to spot objects that the eye cannot see. Our part of the convoy proceeded on its way, this being Thursday, 2nd.December 1943 but, unlike the previous days, we had 'action stations' between midnight and 4am. on Friday, and three Russian Minesweepers and two destroyers joined us at 3.30am. 'Action Stations' entailed all the crew members manning prearranged positions such as gun crews, Radar and Asdic operations, control positions, torpedo operations, look-out positions etc. It continued to snow on Friday as we reached the River Dvina entrance, but it was the thick fog that forced us to anchor outside. The fog lifted on Saturday and we proceeded up the river to the oiler but, as the fog returned as we left the tanker, we had to anchor again. Leaving the River Dvina, we enjoyed some lovely weather and calm seas, but the nights were cold and daylight

Arctic fog. It gives the impression of a boiling sea, due to the difference in air and sea temperatures. (IWM. A15356)

was now from 6am to 2pm. I was on duty during the First Watch, 8pm until midnight, my favourite watch other than the 'Dog Watches', (4pm. to 6pm. and 6pm. to 8pm.), because a reasonable period of sleep was possible after the Watch. The convoy continued on its way on Monday, reaching Veanga Bay on Tuesday at 8am. with the weather very cold and accompanied by snowstorms. The cold was a dry cold that made it more bearable. We oiled and then tied up to the jetty at 2 o'clock in the afternoon, the day ending with Tombola, followed by a bath. At least that was the idea but, in spite of there being three inches of snow and bitterly cold, the Motor Boat was lowered to transport 'Jimmy' and 'Subby' (Sub-Lieutenant Colin MacMillan) to some Russian Destroyers, one of which they boarded. My memory of the Russian destroyer was that it was larger than the 'Beagle'. The Russian sailors invited us aboard and offered us raw fish, bread rissole (coarse brown bread) and real, neat Vodka! As we sat in their mess deck on long wooden benches alongside a long table, we endeavoured to make conversation.

This proved to be somewhat difficult, the Russians having very little English and we having no Russian. After making three more trips to the Russian destroyers, the last one being at half past midnight on Tuesday, we were invited to our own Wardroom for a tot of whisky which we certainly needed to combat the snow and the cold. I am led to believe that, when we had finished our fraternisation with the crew of the Russian Destroyer, it was my duty as Motor Boat coxswain to return

North Russian Arctic landscape and the ships of a convoy. (IWM. A15400)

our crew and officers to the 'Beagle'. I was told at a 31st. re-union of the 3B Club (HM Ships, Beagle, Boadicea & Bulldog 1939-1945 Crews Association), held in the Royal Naval Club in Portsmouth Dockyard, HMS Nelson on 31st. August 1997, that the journey back to HMS Beagle was not a conventional one! One of the officers on the trip to the Russian Destroyer was a Sub-Lieutenant Colin McMillan, now Lieutenant Commander McMillan, RN., and he assured me that, because of the powerful effect of the neat vodka that, as coxswain of the Motor Boat and under my guidance, instead of proceeding directly to the 'Beagle' in a straight line, I adopted a kind of flattened corkscrew pattern, a series of progressive circles, with each one enabling us to advance closer to our destination, HMS Beagle. Oddly enough, there is no note of this unusual experience in my Diary due, no doubt, to the fact that I was somewhat inebriated, and thus it was expunged from my memory when sobriety returned. I had completely forgotten that it had ever happened. Colin, of course, recounted the story with typical naval enthusiasm and I have to rely on him for its veracity. Knowing Colin McMillan, I am sure it must have happened. It is with some regret that my memory does not let me recall the episode, thus enabling me to savour it anew, as it defied all that was traditional in Naval discipline, especially in wartime. It could have resulted in serious repercussions had it not been that everyone involved was in a similar state to myself. In a letter following the reunion, Colin ends with the following paragraph: "I hope that you obtained your Russian gong! You certainly earned it, not least by the volume of vodka you were 'forced' to consume in the line of duty!'

We were certainly beginning to appreciate the Arctic clothing with which we had been issued for the 'Russian Convoy experience', and this included duffle coats, sea boots, woollen jerseys, head coverings and gloves for exterior purposes, but not forgetting the daily rum issue for interior warmth and sustenance. Rum was usually taken neat ('neaters') on the smaller ships such as the 'Beagle'. It was still snowing on Thursday and we made two more trips to the Russian destroyers. I went ashore at 8pm. and saw the film 'Life begins with Andy Hardy' with Mickey Rooney and Judy Garland, although I cannot remember anything about it! There was another trip to the Russian destroyers at 7.20pm. the water proving to be very rough, so rough in fact that it became too risky for the Motor Boat to make the return trip at 10pm. This resulted in us having to walk round by land to the 'Beagle', with it sleeting and blowing a gale – for some reason we were accompanied by some dogs? On Saturday we had to walk back to the Russians to collect the Engineering Office and Sub-Lieutenant Glover, with the gale and the sleet still making life very difficult, to say nothing of the stark landscape, rocky and icy. The gale got steadily worse in the afternoon, so much so that 'Beagle' had to be secured with two more 'lines', steel cables. Nothing of moment happened during the evening, but at 2am. the following morning, 'hands' were called to add another 'wire' for extra security.

On Sunday the Motor Boat was hoisted and, during the afternoon, we went ashore to the hospital to see a ship's concert which was quite good and which

Winter convoys face hard weather. Crew members clearing frozen snow from the forecastle. Convoys carrying vital supplies of food and war equipment sailed under hard winter conditions. This picture was taken on board a destroyer on winter convoy duty. (IWM. A15404)

included a melodrama called 'The Ghost of Bellowing Manor'. We were due to go to sea at 6pm. but this was delayed until 7pm. the following day, which enabled me to have a bath and turn in early. We left Kola Inlet at 9am. on Monday, 13th.December 1943 and travelled at 24 knots, which proved to be pretty bumpy, even though the sea was far from rough. At 6.20pm we met a convoy of four merchantmen and four escorts which had left Dvina River and, with them, proceeded back to the Kola Inlet. In spite of a gale blowing up at 1am. we arrived at midday, oiled and anchored at 3.15pm. We were at sea again at 4pm. and this time travelling at a speed of 17 knots and, although a gale blew up again at 2 o'clock in the morning, we reached the Dvina River at teatime, staying all night. On Thursday it remained very cold and the merchant ships were unable to move being covered with tons of ice and snow. These impediments, common to all vessels in this climate, including ourselves, was a real hazard because it made them unseaworthy., both from the point of view of operating exposed machinery, but also because it made ships unstable. The ice had to be chipped away manually, a desperately thankless task and had to be done repeatedly until we reached warmer temperatures. At 8pm. I started Watch using the Radar 271 set to look for merchant ships that were ready to move and some of them were. The 271 set was closed down at 1am on Friday and we weighed anchor at 9am. collecting a convoy at midday, thereafter making for Kola Inlet at 9-12 knots, the convoy consisting of six merchant ships and three escorts, 'Beagle, Huzzar and Halcyon'. Saturday was a bright day but still very cold and we found three more escorts, but the gale had driven us seven miles off course. Now, with the 271 Radar set broken down, we had to revert to the 291 set. On Sunday, another pleasant day, nothing unusual occurred, except that the 291 set broke down at 6.30pm.- the Radar department was in the dog-house! The breakdown lasted for 3hrs.

We had expected to arrive at Kola Inlet at 5am. but eventually anchored in Veanga Bay at 7am. on Monday, 20th.December, oiled and anchored. There was a 'buzz' going the rounds that the German Battleship 'Tirpitz' was at sea! The Motor Boat was lowered at 9am. and hoisted at 4.15pm. during which time, partly because it was very windy, life was somewhat difficult, the weather having a marked affect on the control of any vessel. The Diary registers the fact that I felt 'chokka' (fed up!). Tuesday was a pleasant day and, as a result, there was an Air Raid alarm at noon, fine weather attracting enemy activity because of good visibility. The M.B. was lowered again at 2pm. with my very good friend, a Scot and my opposite number (in charge of the other Watch) as coxswain, and it was hoisted at teatime, after which I did some dhobying. We weighed anchor on Wednesday at 9am. and waited outside Veanga Bay for a convoy to muster, little knowing what momentous a situation would develop, with us virtually observing from the side-lines, as our convoy made its way back to England.

The exercise of building up a convoy takes time, bearing in mind the number and variety of ships that were used to transport arms and equipment to North Russia, enabling the Russians to continue their fight against the Germans. Fortunately the weather was fine and at noon the convoy started on its way to the UK. There were two convoys at sea at the time engaged in the Russian trips (of which there were many) one, JW55B, proceeding to North Russia, and ours, *Convoy RA55A, (see Appendix B)* proceeding in the opposite direction. Fair weather on Thursday saw a convoy of a couple of dozen merchantmen, protected by fourteen escorts and accompanied by three cruisers which seemed to be 'knocking about' with apparently no particular brief but to carry out duties when and where it was deemed necessary. In spite of the good weather we had no luck whilst trying 'oil ship' (take on oil from the tanker). On Friday the sea became somewhat rougher and, because of U-boat scares, depth charges were dropped, but not by the 'Beagle'.

We sang carols in the evening, Christmas Day being nigh. Saturday, 24th.December 1943 saw the start of the most dramatic episode in the life of HMS Beagle while I was on board as a member of the crew. At 4.30am. our RDF (Radar) 'pinged' what we thought were U-boats in the vicinity of the convoy and we fired star shells (used to illuminate a target) dropping depth charges, but to no avail. We were, of course, at 'Action Stations' throughout situations such as this, and 'Jock' and I would be huddled in the RDF Cabin with barely enough room for both of us. The weather worsened dramatically and the convoy speed was reduced to 6 knots. Several factors played a part in the safety of the Russian Convoys, with the slower speed making it easier for U-boats to target their prey, but the rougher weather making it more difficult to steady the subs to enable them to fire torpedoes accurately. Fog, of course, made it difficult for every-one, but it shielded the ships of the convoy from the deadly, under-water menace. The Christmas meal consisted of corned beef, potatoes and peas, followed by rice pudding, 'yum'!! A daunting problem existed - there was no bread for tea! There was something of the Christmas spirit amongst the crew in spite of the difficult conditions on board, made more uncomfortable by the unfriendly seas. Ships like the 'Beagle' were tossed about like corks, the pitching and tossing combining to make most things difficult, including getting about the vessel. Another problem that Mother Nature threw at ships in Northern climes was the presence of ice, formed by waves breaking over the ship and freezing, making the deck slippery and equipment unusable. The heavy seas were crashing over the deck and pouring down to the mess decks, speed still 12 knots.

CHAPTER NINE

THE 'SCHARNHORST' EPISODE

A terrifying gale developed, creating heavy seas with waves as big as houses and bigger, and this caused 'Beagle' to roll alarmingly. Throughout my naval career I was always happier when the ship that I was on was 'pitching', that is ploughing into the waves head on, rather than being side on to the waves which resulted in 'rolling', probably because I had a fear of the ship 'turning turtle', thus trapping everyone inside. The ships of the convoy were 'all over the place', finding it difficult to steer a steady course, some finding it more difficult than others.

A lasting memory of my time on the 'Beagle' is the infinite power of Nature, the ice and snow, the fog, the cold but, most of all, the sea and its effects on the ships large and small that made up the convoys to and from North Russia. Only those who have had first hand experience can picture the North Atlantic scene, when ships in the convoys were momentarily lost from sight as they sank into the troughs of the waves, only to be hoisted high on the brow of another wave, one minute the bows of merchantmen ploughing into Neptune's seas, causing their sterns to be raised

A merchant ship coping with heavy weather. (IWM. A27565)

heavenwards, their screws (propellers) thrashing the empty air and next, with their bows lifted, crashing into another wave peak. 'Beagle' often shuddered from stem to stern. At one moment the ships of the convoy were visible, vanishing from sight the next, only to appear again in all their glory.

An enduring feeling, and an unsettling one, was when 'Beagle', having climbed to the peak of a wave, seemed to hover endlessly before descending into the wall of water awaiting. One wondered, at times, how vessels survived the onslaught, as most of them did; thankfully, there were mitigating circumstances, when the awful conditions were relieved by the occasional, contrasting calm seas and harbours of relative serenity. As I mentioned earlier, it was sometimes impossible to maintain convoy discipline, with some ships unable to sustain speed and direction and losing out to unequal struggle, causing them to become stragglers and thus losing escort protection. This made them possible targets to underwater marauders, although life was equally difficult for U-boats when it came to firing torpedoes accurately.

The speed of the convoy was now 12 knots in spite of the bad weather and, on this day, Sunday, 26th.December, we left with the destroyer 'Athabascan' at noon to investigate something suspicious, I cannot remember what. The gale was abating and, at 8am enemy surface craft were spotted, resulting in three cruisers and four destroyers (not 'Beagle') being despatched to intercept. Contact was lost after the initial sighting, but regained at 11am and the 'Duke of York' made for the position. Incidentally, the cruiser 'Norfolk' had been hit aft in this skirmish. Contact was lost again between 4pm and 5pm, but was re-established by Radar at a distance of 12,000 yards. Star shells (a method of lighting up the target) were fired, but at this stage 'cat and mouse' tactics were the order of the day. Ships were chasing each other around in circles! By 6pm. the gale was increasing again and by this time, due to the hammering we were experiencing from the rough seas, we had no hot water for washing (the VAP, the machine for creating fresh water from sea water, was out of order), a dynamo was also out of order, and we were steaming on one of the two boilers which, of course, affected our speed. As a result of these difficulties, water was reserved for just drinking and cooking and washing-up had to be done with salt water! On top of all this, we had to bear the depravation of no bread for tea! Another effect of the formidable seas, with 'Beagle' ploughing into the waves was, that as the sea water crashed over the bows and the ship as a whole, it poured down to the mess decks, thus creating a depth of water in our living quarters, something we had to live with throughout the Russian convoy trips. Naturally, we were never able to get dry and it was miraculous that more of the crew were not ill. I suppose that we adapted to the conditions both physically and mentally and our bodies responded positively, helped by the daily demands expected of us as protectors of the seaman and valuable cargoes being transported in the merchantmen.

It was still Sunday, 26th.December 1943 and at 1800 (6pm.) THE 'SCHARNHORST' WAS ON FIRE, and by 2000 (8pm.) THE 'SCHARNHORST' WAS SUNK. (For a fuller description of the sinking of the 'Scharnhorst' and details of all the Russian Convoys, names of merchant ships and escorts, cargoes transported etc., the reader can do no better than refer to Richard Woodman's book, 'Arctic Convoys', first published by John Murray (Publishers) Ltd. in 1994. Another book worth consulting is one by Bob Ruegg and Arnold Hague entitled 'Convoys to Russia' (1941-1945) published in 1992.) To round off the day we had 'Action Stations' from 9.15pm to 9.30pm and this was due to a U-boat scare, triggered off by an RDF contact with no recorded result and probably a false alarm.

There must have been countless examples of fate taking a hand by creating instances which, in themselves might appear small, but which had or could have had a considerable effect on the historical development of World War II. Some could have been the result of luck or ill luck, but others might have been ineffective leadership?

Russia- Descriptions

Contemporary background information about two of the places visited by HMS Beagle during its tour of duty as a destroyer escorting convoys from the U.K. to North Russia and back. The descriptions of the places are as they were during the 1940's, at the time of the writing of the Diary.

KOLA: Capital of Russian Lapland in the peninsula of North Russia of the same name, between the White Sea and the Arctic Ocean. It was coterminous with the Murmansk region of R.S.F.S.R., and included most of Russian Lapland. The north shore was called the 'Murman', i.e. Norman coast. The countryside was mainly dreary and inhospitable and, before the Soviet five-year plans, was inhabited on the coast only. Power for the big hydro-electric scheme was derived from the river Niva. The peninsula came into the news with the Allied expedition to the Murman coast in 1918. Its small population was mainly engaged in fishing. (The Kola Inlet became important during the Second World War as a reception area for convoys supplying the Russian armed forces with war materials).

MURMANSK: An Arctic city and seaport of the U.S.S.R. On the Kola Inlet of the Murmansk coast, it owed its development to the Murman railway, which directly linked it with Leningrad. Murmansk harbour was ice-free throughout the year, unlike Archangel, and the town had a fishing industry and a trade in fish products. (Murmansk was a terminal port for convoys from Great Britain and the U.S.A. during the Second World War).

CHAPTER TEN

RETURN TO 'BLIGHTY'

It does not bear thinking about what might have happened had the 'Scharnhorst' not been sunk, with two convoys at sea at her mercy, although she would have been thwarted in no uncertain terms by the convoy escorts, including ourselves of course!

On Monday, 27th. the gale subsided a little between midnight and breakfast time, but the respite was short lived with the weather becoming worse than ever in the afternoon. So much so that we had to 'heave to' (take the 'way'- forward movement- off the ship and try to keep the bow into the waves to avoid 'rolling') in order to accommodate the change of 'Watch'. Changing a 'Watch' consisted of one group of members of the crew taking over he duties of those who had been on duty during the previous four hours. 'Heaving to' didn't obviate 'pitching' although it did modify this consistently uncomfortable motion. Had we not 'heaved to', crew movement about the ship would have been endangered, if not impossible, in spite of ropes being fixed the length of the ship to hold on to. Not much sleep was had by anyone and, because there were some of the crew on duty aft, it fell to me to take them some hot tea to warm them up. Unfortunately, with the ship 'rolling', I managed to tip the tea all over me but fortunately, because of the thick and heavy clothing necessary for protection from the cold, I was not scalded.

The photograph opposite is that of a Royal Navy Cruiser (far larger than a destroyer!) and the following description (gleaned from an Imperial War Museum report associated with the picture) graphically describes Neptune at its worst: ' The British Cruiser had a battle with the elements during a passage through Northern waters. She ran into storms of great severity, which lasted for three days. At times the wind reached hurricane force of more than 65 knots (about 75 m.p.h.). Driving spray formed a curtain, which reduced visibility to less than a cable (200 yards). So great was the wind pressure on her hull and upper works that she was hove to, with engines running at minimum speed to give steerage way. Heavy seas stove in the starboard whaler and hurled an accommodation ladder from its sea stowage to the quarter-deck. Depth charges, smoke floats and Carley rafts went overboard. After three days the storm abated with surprising suddenness and the Cruiser was able to set course for port'. The picture was taken when waves more than 50 feet high were crashing on the deck of the Cruiser.

On Tuesday 28th.December I had the 'Middle Watch', but with the weather still bad and with the 'Beagle' pitching and tossing, life was uncomfortable for all. There was still no water with which to wash and the mess decks were swimming with salt water. This and the fact that the mess deck was leaking, made home comforts seem a lifetime away. The wind dropped slightly between 10pm. and midnight but, in

The North Atlantic at its worst. (IWM. A14892)

Difficult weather conditions encountered during action with U-boats. (IWM. A13374)

spite of the seas being still somewhat heavy, we maintained a speed of 12 knots. News was received from HMS Glasgow regarding the sighting of four German Destroyers, always lurking in these northern seas, but no further details were forthcoming. On top of the discomforts already mentioned, our 271 (Radar) cabin was also leaking. It seemed that nothing could be made watertight, including the ship, in these ferocious conditions. Rain and sleet were making visibility difficult and this was when Radar was invaluable. I turned in after the First Watch but did not get to sleep until 4am. or thereabouts. It was damp and very cold in the mess deck accommodation and I had to cover myself with an extra Duffle coat whilst sleeping in my hammock, to maintain some semblance of warmth. Hammocks comprised the sleeping accommodation on board small naval ships during the war. Hammocks remained slung during rough weather and also whilst in action for obvious reasons, but this made for difficulties moving about the 'mess'.

The gale was still strong on Wednesday 29th. but the day was fairly bright. We consumed half a tin of steak and kidney pie for lunch, accompanied by a couple of ship's biscuits! We obviously benefited from *cordon bleu* cooking! The speed of the convoy remained at a steady 12 knots and in spite of there being no water with which to wash, we cleaned up the mess deck to the best of our abilities. Jock, my opposite number (i.e. in charge of the other 'watch' and also a Leading Seaman) and I went aft to the store for more pies and biscuits, not easy under the difficult conditions. The 'Beagle' reached the Faroes at 10pm. where we anchored for the night, with the weather continuing to be snowy and windy. At 9am. we went alongside the oil tanker, with the 'Cockatrice' tied up to us and 'Athabascan' and 'Ashanti' on the other side of the oiler.

The crew of the 'Athabascan' had their Christmas, being unable to celebrate it whilst at sea owing to the rough weather. We took on stores, after which I had a bath – at last! On Friday, 31st.December we remained alongside with little to do, but we were pleased to be free from the rough weather and mountainous seas, the continuous, desperately uncomfortable movement of the ship whilst at sea (it took a little time to regain our sea-legs) short rations, lack of water, and a mess deck that was more or less normal and free of slung hammocks, and considerably drier than it had been for some time. Some of our crew took a little time to adapt to the new conditions and got drunk on 'sippers' (rum).

CHAPTER ELEVEN

1944 AND A NEW YEAR

On Saturday, 1st.January we made for Greenock, arriving at 9.45am. We had travelled at 27 knots - I think the Captain as well as the crew had been anxious to get to Greenock, with the prospect of home leave. The journey had taken us through the Minches, with fair weather but the sea creating a swell (long undulating waves) making the trip a little uncomfortable, not that anybody cared! We were in Greenock, Glasgow and Gourock etc. from 1st.January until 18th.February whilst 'Beagle' was brought back to A1 condition. She had suffered, as I mentioned earlier, and equipment etc. had to be repaired and serviced. The crew enjoyed fourteen days leave during this time, eventually returning aboard to make sure 'Beagle' was 'shipshape and Bristol fashion', ready for the next convoy to Russia. On Friday, 18th. February we left Greenock for a 'shoot' which, presumably, was to get the crew back into shape, after which we made for Loch Ewe, arriving there on Saturday at 9am.

The Motor Boat was lowered although it was very windy and this resulted in us suffering from plenty of spray. I was off duty during the afternoon and the evening, and the following day, Sunday, we proceeded to the oil tanker at 2pm. the day being a lovely one. The Motor Boat was hoisted inboard at 1.30pm. and we left Loch Ewe at 6.30pm. with a convoy of forty merchantmen and twenty escorts, *Convoy JW57*

Ships of a British convoy stretching as far as the eye can see. (IWM. HU62804)

(see Appendix C), a much larger group of ships than the last one, to make another hazardous trip to Russia. Much was made of the success of this convoy, described as the largest sent to Russia. The convoy was accompanied by several war correspondents who were 'with the Home Fleet in Northern Waters'. At some future date, 'Beagle' was to actually have war correspondents on board, but that is another story. (For more information about this convoy, see Richard Woodman's book, 'Arctic Convoys'). The initial speed was, not uncommonly, 12 knots and we continued at the same speed on Monday, 21st.February(my birthday) the day being fine with bright sunshine, although it was pretty cold. Speed was dictated by the size and content of the convoy and the weather, with sufficient speed to avoid U-boat attacks and also conducive to the conservation of fuel supplies, the speed of the slowest merchantman being paramount. Tuesday was another pleasant day with sunshine but with some mist, the weather deteriorating later with a gale springing up, not enough however to make the sea particularly rough. It remained pretty cold in spite of the sunshine.

Wednesday was still windy, but as the sun continued to shine the wind force dropped slightly, still leaving us cold but providing the ideal conditions for submarine attack! In fact we became aware that we were being shadowed. Thursday saw the inevitable start of bread rationing. 'Beagle' was now iced up, with ice everywhere, making difficult conditions worse. Added to this it was very windy with rough seas throwing water all over the ship, the water freezing solid as soon as it touched any surface. Enemy aircraft and U-boats forced us to adopt 'Action Stations', during which we managed to dodge a torpedo, either as the result of the good eyesight of the lookouts or the Asdic operators. Whatever the reason, the safety of the ship was ultimately reliant on the quick, intelligent response and experience of the Captain and he was to show these attributes on several more occasions.

We continued to be shadowed on Friday, the weather conditions continuing to be windy and rough and, as the day developed, increased activity involving enemy aircraft and subs made it necessary for us to adopt three more 'Action Stations', depth charges being dropped during the forenoon with no evident success. Whilst we were at 'Action Stations' again at 9pm, HMS Mahratta was torpedoed twice and, with the 'Impulsive' standing by to give any help possible (there was very little hope for survivors in the ice-cold water) we departed from our escort position to investigate hopefully to find the U-boat responsible, but again without success. Because of further action, we managed about two hours sleep, although cat-nap would be more appropriate! We thought that we had sunk an enemy submarine during the night, but there was no irrefutable proof, and we managed to dodge two more torpedoes! sometimes try to recall how I felt during these Russian trips, especially those crammed with incident and, although my feelings and responses are different from those nearly sixty years ago, I am the same person. I think it would be fair to say that there were some feelings of anticipation and apprehension, but we were so caught up in the 'actions' that I have described, that the adrenaline took over, resulting in positive thinking that left no space for negative thoughts. The problems and discomfort described during our first convoy were no less this time, in fact we now had water in the fan shafts, and the mess deck was flooded as were the lockers that contained our belongings, clothing etc. All this was due to our high-speed activities chasing the enemy, regardless of the rough seas.

On Saturday, 26th.February 1944 we were involved in more action during the morning, with a submarine spotted on the surface, but we were not involved in following this up. We dodged further torpedoes and, on top of everything being flooded, there was no water with which to wash. On re-reading my Diary, I found it frightening to read how many torpedoes we managed to dodge, but at 6am. on Sunday there were more 'Action Stations', during which we had to dodge more torpedoes! The weather was very, very cold, with ice all over the ship, inside and outside. Tons of depth charges were dropped during action in the forenoon and oil was seen on the surface of the sea but we were not able to confirm that it was coming from a damaged submarine. We spent considerable time chipping away ice from everything, hard work and not very reward-ing but very necessary. Monday was a better day, nice and calm, but still cold and we arrived at Kola Inlet in Northern Russia at 9pm. tying up alongside an oil tanker. I was able to 'turn in' at 11.30pm. but, with the clocks advanced two hours because of time zones, had to get up at 7.30am. on Tuesday morning. We remained in Kola Inlet for the whole of Tuesday and I had to cope with an iced up Motor Boat - was I fed up! Although the M.B. was still in the same condition on Wednesday, but not quite so badly affected by the ice, we managed to get the engine started at 5pm. Films were shown on board that evening. Thursday meant another morning trip to the oiler and, after putting the clocks back two hours, we left Kola Inlet at 2.30pm.

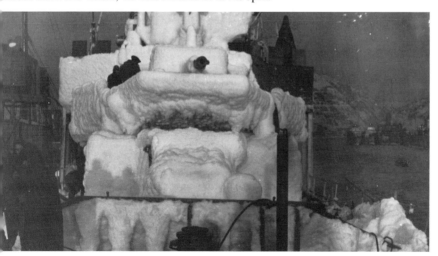

Looking aft from the forecastle. A lot of snow had already been cleared when this picture was taken. (IWM. AX97A).

CHAPTER TWELVE

MORE RUSSIAN CONVOYS

We escorted an oil tanker to join a homeward bound *Convoy RA57* (see 'Arctic Convoys) made up of twenty six merchantmen, twenty three escorts, two AA Cruisers and an Aircraft Carrier. On Friday the weather was pretty bad and we took a position on the starboard bow of the convoy. Two U-boats were sunk by Swordfish planes and it was proved time and time again how invaluable these planes were in the fight against German submarines, the pilots being able to spot the subs from the air, often taking them by surprise. Planes linking up with escort warships proved to be even more successful, as we were to find out during a later convoy. The destroyer HMS Onslaught picked up survivors from the sunken subs and we were sure that another U-boat had been damaged as a result of dropping further tons of depth charges. On Saturday the weather had improved but, unfortunately, a merchant ship was sunk, albeit with all 'hands' saved. Sunday, another fine day, saw more success against the enemy in the shape of two more U-boats sunk by Swordfish aircraft during the morning. U-boats were still loafing around on Monday, the lovely weather possibly making them more adventurous. Successes (so far) against the enemy during the course of this convoy included eight U-boats sunk and four damaged. In fact the successes became more frequent as the year wore on, due to better intelligence, better organisation and, probably, fewer U-boats available to attack the convoys, so many having been sunk. On Tuesday and Wednesday we were blessed with more fair weather, but there were no further incidents and we left the convoy at 11am on the Wednesday.

We reached Scapa Flow the following day to drop off two sick members of the crew, proceeding on to Greenock and reaching there at 9am. on Friday. The ship's company departed on a much welcomed leave at 12.30pm. on Friday, 10th.March, the leave lasting until midnight on the 17th. We were based at Greenock and Gourock etc., between 18th. and 26th.March. On Monday, 27th.March we made for the Faroes with destroyers 'Keppel, Boadicea and Walker', and this took us through Tuesday and Wednesday, when we reached our destination at 9am and anchored. The Motor Boat was lowered at 10am and hoisted inboard again at 1.30pm, the crew having carried out all the tasks for which they were needed. We went alongside the oiler at 2pm. shore leave being granted between 4pm. and 6pm. but there was little of interest ashore.

At 4am. (more unsocial hours!!) on Thursday, 30th.March we joined a convoy travelling at 9 knots, consisting of fifty five merchant ships and forty one escorts, an even larger convoy than the last two, to make another trip to Northern Russia. The weather was quite good, enabling us to oil at sea, that is to take on oil whilst still 'under way'. This was *Convoy JW58* (see 'Arctic Convoys') and the organisation necessary to the bringing about of the meeting together of such an 'armada' involved a huge naval operation. It was a response by the Western Allies to the continuing advance of the Red Army, which had now cleared the Germans out of the Ukraine and was approaching the Crimea and the Carpathians, prior to a drive into Poland. There was no excitement on Friday and the weather, which continued to be good, carried over into Saturday when, unfortunately, an aircraft crashed on to an Aircraft Carrier, possibly the 'Tracker', presumably while it was trying to land on the carrier's flight deck. Landing on an aircraft carrier was difficult at the best of times but, with the flight deck rising and falling, judging the height of the aircraft in relation to the deck needed great skill and experience.

The landings had to be a joint venture, with the carrier heading into the wind and sailing in the right direction at the right speed, and with a member of the aircraft carrier crew (armed with coloured bats, rather like the airport personnel who help to direct pilots of planes to park at their allotted places) directing the pilot of the aircraft to move the plane up or down or to the right or to the left and indicating when to touch down. Crashes were inevitable at times, especially in rough weather. We oiled again and, not uncommon on this trip, were at 'Action Stations' all day because of the vicinity of enemy submarines. Sunday was another lovely day, which was an advantage as far as the U-boats were concerned, torpedoes being more likely to find their targets if the 'sub' is reasonably still at the time of firing and visibility good, but it meant that we were at 'Action Stations' from twelve minutes past midnight until 2am. U-boats were observed on the surface, which was rather worrying because they can travel more quickly on the surface and manoeuvre more easily. At 4pm. an aircraft crashed into the sea and so we rushed at a speed of 30 knots to the area, and were able to pick up the pilot at 5.30pm.(Appendix I). This was in spite of there being two U-boats on the surface and German aircraft (Bloh & Voss 138) snooping. On Monday we spent all day chasing subs all over the ocean without success, but the weather continued to be fine and we discovered that the airman, picked up yesterday, was OK.

On the way to Kola Inlet on another lovely, calm day we sank a mine, arriving at 5pm. and anchoring, with a sigh of relief, because most if not all the convoy had arrived safely. At 8pm. we tied up alongside the oiler and the clocks were advanced two hours again. The airman that we had picked up came aboard and gave a talk about what it was like to be a pilot on an aircraft carrier. During the forenoon of Wednesday the Motor Boat was lowered and 'Beagle' went alongside the destroyer 'Saumerez, which in turn was tied up to the 'Diadem'. I was coxswain of the M.B. from 12.30pm. until 10pm. a matter of nine and a half hours with hardly a break, except for just enough time for supper, with the last trip at 11pm ending at 2am on Thursday morning! On Tuesday forenoon it fell to my lot to take on the duties of Coxswain again, but I was free during the afternoon and evening and spent it dhobying and playing the piano accordion, a brand new 120 bass Hohner

A convoy of ships in Arctic waters. (IWM. A15421)

instrument which I had discovered (unused) in the Radio Transmission Room. Knowing quite a bit about music, it did not take me long to master the bass buttons played by the left hand and, being a pianist, the right-hand technique was straightforward enough, albeit the keyboard being at a different angle from a pianoforte. I eventually 'hit the sack' (went to bed – hammock) at 10.30pm. and, with the clocks put back one hour during the night, had to rise at 7am.on the following day, Friday, 7th.April to hoist the Motor Boat prior to the 'Beagle' visiting the oiler.

At 9am. we secured for sea and proceeded with another large convoy of ships consisting of forty five merchantmen and forty(?) escorts in a homeward bound direction on what was to be a fairly uneventful trip. I think most probably that Hitler's U-boats, if they had any priorities, would have concentrated on convoys going to Russia heavily laden with war equipment, rather than convoys returning to the UK with less important cargoes in terms of the war effort. This was *Convoy RA58* (see 'Arctic Convoys') and we started the trip enjoying lovely weather, but on Saturday it became very cold with snow. The sea was a still calm and the pleasant weather returned for Sunday, Monday and Tuesday but again this was ideal weather for U-boat attacks and we were aware of their presence. Later in the day (Tuesday) we left the convoy with destroyers 'Keppel, Diadem and Walker' travelling at 18 knots, with a windy morning and a fair afternoon.

We reached Scapa Flow during the forenoon of Thursday, where we spent Friday until Tuesday and, as I was Motor Boat Coxswain from 12.30pm. on Saturday, it fell to me to transport drunken officers around until 2am the following day!! We left Scapa Flow at 6am on Wednesday, 19th.April and I must say for my part with some relief as for me it seemed to be more peaceful at sea than in harbour for the reasons indicated! We arrived at the Faroes again at 6pm and left four hours later to pick up other ships at 1am. This was not a convoy as such there being no merchantmen, in fact we travelled at 16 knots in the company of two aircraft carriers, one cruiser and 20 destroyers, with pleasant weather and nothing of incident to report. The reason for sending this 'fleet' (see Appendix G) to Russia was to collect a number of empty merchant ships lying in Russian ports and use them to transport home the 1,336 crew of USS Milwaukee (which had been handed over to the Russians for repatriation) together with 1,430 Russian sailors, who would serve on British warships as they awaited transfer to the Red Fleet. The personnel ship 'Nea Hellas' was the only non-naval vessel to sail with this 'fleet', but unfortunately it developed defects and had to return to the UK, thus depriving the large Russian contingent of Transport. After a swift re-organisation by the British Staff in Northern Russia, they were dispersed among the naval ships and the empty cargo vessels, the unusual cargo taking the form of Officers and Ratings. (see 'Convoys to Russia' for details of the personnel and their dispersal amongst the Navy ships and the Merchant ships.)

Preparations for the Operation 'Neptune' (the invasion of Normandy) precluded running further JW convoys (convoys to Russia) at this time, and it was decided to pass this strong escort group through Kola Inlet in the shortest possible time to retrieve those ships still there as well as personnel. Friday saw quite good weather with nothing happening worthy of mention, except that we sank three mines. On Saturday, 22nd.April we started to pitch badly due to the change in the weather, strong winds and freezing temperatures developing. Our course was altered to 075 degrees, and on Sunday the sea flattened slightly enabling us to sink two more mines. We reached Kola Inlet at 9pm. tied up alongside the cruiser 'Diadem' two hours later, transferring to the oiler at 4am. on Monday. As I mentioned earlier, the Royal Navy was oblivious of the time of day it was, or the comfort of the crew, but this was understandable (when one thinks rationally) the expeditious ending of the war taking precedent over most things. Monday proved to be another lovely day, we were lucky on this trip so far, and I had a bath, followed by some dhobying. We were paid, and this involved one of the Royal Naval rituals necessitating queuing up and, when we reached the Officer responsible, doffing one's cap, stating one's number, reinstating the cap and marching away! We spent Tuesday and Wednesday alongside the oil tanker and on Thursday, still alongside, we enjoyed a concert on board the oiler. It was quite enjoyable.

Friday saw the last day of our visits to the 'North' and, leaving the tanker at 9.30am. we proceeded to sea at midday with one of the largest convoys for which we carried out escort duties, consisting of fifty four merchantmen, twenty three escorts, 2 aircraft carriers and one cruiser. Our speed was 9 knots and the weather

A general view of a convoy showing a near miss (bomb). In the foreground there is an escort destroyer travelling at speed. (IWM. A12022)

was fine, although there was some snow. The snow together with fine weather was repeated on Saturday and the day was quiet with a calm sea. This was our last *Convoy RA59* (see 'Arctic Convoys') and we enjoyed another lovely day on Sunday, the last day of April. The peaceful trip, with the continuing speed of 9 – 10 knots, was shattered, with a merchant ship being torpedoed – we watched it 'go up in smoke' as it broke into two pieces. Fortunately most of the 163 members of the crew were picked up.

Throughout the war I never ceased to be affected by the loss of life, particularly when it was due to the sinking of one of our convoy's escorts or one of the merchant ships, the latter being so helpless, with their great hulks having few armaments and no great speed or manoeuvrability. Survival in the icy waters of the North Atlantic was almost impossible, especially if the water was contaminated with fuel oil from the damaged or sinking ship, any situation being made worse if an oil tanker was torpedoed. We chased U-boats and dropped depth charges and Mk10's(?) with no appreciable results. On instruction from the Commodore we moved our position from the starboard quarter to the port quarter of the convoy and, being at the rear we were, as far as I can remember, able to stream 'foxers', these consisting of lengths of metallic material(?) streamed out aft of 'Beagle' to fox the enemy by confusing their transmissions and torpedoes. Monday was another lovely day with subs still loafing, but a wind sprang up and we had a few flakes of snow. It was calm enough for me to have a bath. Tuesday was very windy, with the sea just rough enough to make things

An ammunition ship exploding. (IWM. A12271)

uncomfortable and with the fine weather making it easier for U-boats to shadow the convoy, although one was sunk by a Swordfish aeroplane. Wednesday was similar to the previous days with the subs in attendance. I practised my seamanship by making a wire strop which meant splicing strands of wire, a task requiring a considerable amount of effort. I enjoyed listening to a recording of Schumann's Piano Concerto played by Myra Hess at 9.15pm. but where I was able to listen to it and on what equipment I can only suggest that it was in the First Lieutenant's cabin or nearby. The weather was fairly quiet with the wind astern which, incidentally, made the 'Beagle' adopt an odd skew-like movement through the water. Thursday greeted us with a marvellous morning of bright sunshine and at 8.25am. I enjoyed listening to a recording of Liszt's First Piano Concerto, an excellent way to start the day. The sea was nice and calm and the wind had dropped. HMS Diadem and a few other escorts, including an aircraft carrier, left the convoy, leaving the 8th. Escort Group, of which 'Beagle' was a part, in charge from that afternoon onwards. In contrast to the daytime, the weather turned rough that night, but with a full moon. In spite of the ship's un-comfortable movement, I was able to listen to a recording of Geraldo as part of the radio series, 'These you have loved'. A full moon usually meant trouble as the U-boats could see their targets more easily, but with the mitigating circumstances of the rough sea, opportunities to torpedo the convoy merchantmen were much reduced. The weather was better on Friday and, although the sea continued to be quite rough, we were able to sink another mine, this being done by gunfire.

On Saturday we sighted land, the welcoming shores of Scotland, but after arriving at Gourock at 8am. we had to wait until 1.30pm. before we could tie up alongside the quay. As usual the Motor Boat was lowered, this being our only physical link between 'Beagle' and land or other ships. During Sunday, Monday and Tuesday we remained at Gourock, with a short leave being granted for the next four days. We arrived back from leave at noon on Monday, 15th.May, followed by exercises in the Clyde from Monday to Thursday, proceeding to Larne, Ireland or Friday. We exercised off Larne in the Irish Sea during Saturday and Sunday returning to Gourock on Monday, and staying until Friday. We left Gourock on Saturday heading for the Solent, reaching there at 10pm. on Sunday, 28th. May and after oiling, we anchored.

As far as I can recollect, we were not aware at that time how near 'D' Day was nor had we any inkling that 'Beagle' would be taking part. How the mammoth preparations were kept from the Hun was a miracle, large areas of England secretly storing invasion equipment and men.

CHAPTER THIRTEEN

THE BEGINNING OF THE END

We remained at anchor during Monday, Tuesday and Wednesday and at 9.15am. we started patrolling. The diary does not state where, but I suspect it was in The English Channel. There was in fact nothing to report, small satisfaction after what had been a rather monotonous exercise and which had lasted until 11.45am. on Friday, the day we arrived back in the Solent. We remained at anchor on Saturday and I was able to go sailing in the clinker-built whaler in the afternoon from 4pm. to 8pm. Sunday was very windy and the waters of the Solent were rough, not an uncommon phenomenon, the troublesome water being partly due to the complicated currents, both ends of the Solent being open to the English Channel. Monday, 5th. June 1944, the original date for the 'Landings', saw us proceeding to sea at 2pm. with some landing barges etc. The sea was somewhat choppy and some of the landing craft turned back, resulting in what we now know was the delay of the Assault on the French Coast until the following day, 'D' Day, 6th. June, a momentous day in the history of World War II and the history of the World! At 4pm. we adopted a system of two 'Watches', one which we had experienced during our trips to Russia, and one which put 'Beagle' in its highest state of alertness. There is an entry in my Diary which states that at 11pm. on 5th.June, 1,100 paratroopers landed on the French Coast, but I was not able to verify this.

CHAPTER FOURTEEN

OPERATION 'OVERLORD'

My diary contains details of the assault on the French Coast, written at the time, but I am not sure of the source – hence the following.

At about 4am. the RAF started bombing beachheads and dropped 4,200 tons of bombs. At 7.10am. the American Air Force (their whole strength) started bombing, which lasted for 15 minutes, the beaches, sand dunes and the defences between Le Havre and Cherbourg. 7 battleships, 93 destroyers and 22 Cruisers carried out a bombardment to cover the landing from 7.40am. until Zero hour, with the British and Canadians to the East and the Americans to the West. About 4,000 craft of all kinds took part in the initial landings, with aircraft marked with white stripes underneath (one night allowed to complete the painting!). The German fleet consisted of 5 destroyers, 60 'E' boats and a good number of U-boats. Groups under the command of Captain Walker etc., patrolled and hunted, to stop U-boats entering the English Channel.

H.M.S. BEAGLE'S PART IN THE ACTION

On the morning of Monday, 6th.June 1944 'Action Stations' were manned at 4am. At 6am. the fleet shelled the French Coast – COLOSSAL! There did not appear to be much resistance. Had we caught old 'Jerry' on back foot? At 7.10am. the Americans bombed the French Coast areas – DRAMATIC! The barge/landing craft reached the coast at 7.30am. and, having been an escort in the invading 'Armada', we proceeded back to 'Pompey'(Portsmouth) at 7.45am. at a speed of 32 knots, the fastest I could remember since joining the 'Beagle', arriving at 10am. During the afternoon the destroyer 'Wrestler' struck a mine.(There were and had been vessels of all shapes and sizes the length and breadth of the English Channel as far as the eye could see.)

The reason that we had sped back to Portsmouth was to pick up some V.I.P's and at 2pm. we left for France with 2 Brigadiers and 2 Captains (there may have been more?). The trip back to France also involved the 'Beagle' speeding at 32 knots and we arrived at our destination at 6pm. There is something very

Troops disembarking from the 'Beagle' and boarding an M.L. for the trip to the beach. (IWM. 23908B)

SUPREME HEADQUARTERS
ALLIED EXPEDITIONARY FORCE

Soldiers, Sailors and Airmen of the Allied Expeditionary Force!

You are about to embark upon the Great Crusade, toward which we have striven these many months. The eyes of the world are upon you. The hopes and prayers of liberty-loving people everywhere march with you. In company with our brave Allies and brothers-in-arms on other Fronts, you will bring about the destruction of the German war machine, the elimination of Nazi tyranny over the oppressed peoples of Europe, and security for ourselves in a free world.

Your task will not be an easy one. Your enemy is well trained, well equipped and battle-hardened. He will fight savagely.

But this is the year 1944! Much has happened since the Nazi triumphs of 1940-41. The United Nations have inflicted upon the Germans great defeats, in open battle, man-to-man. Our air offensive has seriously reduced their strength in the air and their capacity to wage war on the ground. Our Home Fronts have given us an overwhelming superiority in weapons and munitions of war, and placed at our disposal great reserves of trained fighting men. The tide has turned! The free men of the world are marching together to Victory!

I have full confidence in your courage, devotion to duty and skill in battle. We will accept nothing less than full Victory!

Good Luck! And let us all beseech the blessing of Almighty God upon this great and noble undertaking.

Dwight D Eisenhower

A message from General Eisenhower given to all those taking part on 'D' Day.

Representing the Combined Press

ABOARD H.M.S. BEAGLE, Off Normandy Beaches, Tuesday.

DAY has come to a close and the Royal Navy has put up one of the finest jobs of the war. They are still doing it.

An endless stream of ships carrying reinforcements of men, tanks, guns, ammunition, continue to come across to France. And conditions have not been easy. Rolling seas, tides, wind and many other factors made landings extremely difficult during first light this morning.

But the men of the Royal Navy somehow managed, and the initial assault and follow-up forces were safely landed on the beaches.

This tough little destroyer Beagle has had an amazing wartime record.

Streaming to beach

We have passed along lines of tank landing craft, motor launches and supply ships steadily streaming towards the beachhead. In the other direction similar groups of ships of all sizes have been steaming for home to bring up more and more reinforcements.

The smaller ships of the Royal Navy have had a very tough time. It was about midnight, just before zero hour on D-Day, that we found our first casualty. We were steaming for the coast of France.

The wind was high and seas were lashing over our bows. A faint light signalled S O S out of the darkness.

Badly holed •

We turned towards it and found a small assault landing craft manned by a Royal Marine second lieutenant, three Marine privates, and three ratings tossing about the sea. She was holed badly up forward.

We pulled them aboard. One of the marine privates had been so seasick that it took the ship's doctor some time to pull him round.

This evening, as we lie at anchor close in to the invasion beaches, the waters of the Baie de la Seine present an even more amazing sight than they did at first light this morning.

Naval craft seem to have increased in number, and the whole area is packed with shipping, cruisers, destroyers, lumbering tanks, landing craft, flying their little barrage balloons from the stern of supply ships. Motor launches, tugs, minesweepers, they are all there.

The seas have now abated, and the sun is shining, lighting up the little seaside resorts. But the beach battle goes on: away to the south-west British destroyers are bombarding

Never known

The R.A.F. and the U.S. Air Force continue to give air support to a degree never before known by an expeditionary force.

Spasmodic black patches of German ack ack speckled the sky. Not once during the whole course of D-Day have we seen or heard a Luftwaffe plane. British and American fighters are never absent.

Flying at varying heights, they have given constant cover.

But the climax to the whole Allied air invasion plan came late this evening at the close of D-day when we watched the second wave of glider-borne troops soaring in over the area.

They came in hundreds in one endless stream, flying at an incredibly low altitude.

HMS Beagle off 'Gold Beach', standing guard over landing craft as they made their way to the French beaches. (IWM. A23872)

HMS Beagle involved with the rescue of Americans from sunk LST's. (IWM. 23974B)

exciting about a destroyer speeding through the waves at speed at any time, but this occasion was heightened by the thought that we involved in activities that could spell the end of World War II. We dropped the army officers on the H.Q. Ship and anchored about four miles off the French coast. Many bombers went over us - I think they were 'Fortresses'.

At 9pm. we returned to England, this time to Portland, at a speed of 12 knots. The Americans were using this seaside resort as a base. Hammocks remained slung during all these activities which was common practice when small naval ships were in action. We reached Portland at 6.30am. on Wednesday, 7th.June, oiled and anchored at 4pm. in Weymouth Bay. After spending the night at anchor we sailed on another trip to France on Thursday and, during the this trip, the ship's company were photographed by Desmond Tighe, the representative of one of the better known newspapers, but there is no note in the Diary of the return journey. I was coxswain of the Motor Boat during the afternoon, enabling the taking of photographs of HMS Beagle (I do not seem to have a copy.) We left England at 3pm. on Thursday with five American LST's (large landing craft) for Omaha Beach and everything went well until 2.21am. on Friday when two of the LST's were torpedoed. We had to chase off some German 'E' boats, fast torpedo boats, nearly ramming a convoy travelling in the opposite direction at 2.30am! One of the LST's blew up at 5am. and we stopped to pick up survivors from the burning vessel. This, unfortunately, meant sailing through a minefield! It was an instant but conscious decision on the part of the Captain and, either because of programmed behaviour established over months serving on the 'Beagle', or because of the crew's confidence in the 'Skipper' (built on the memory of his skill in avoiding torpedoes and mines etc.) we entered into this highly dangerous exercise with a certain amount of trepidation but, more importantly, with an overwhelming desire to save as many American sailors as possible. There were 150 survivors. Sadly, on the way back to Portsmouth, we had to bury (at sea) 12 of the American crew. The survivors were in Carley Floats and smaller landing craft that had been on board the larger LST, many of them injured. We got them on board as best we could, mostly by lowering nets over the side, with crew members hanging on to them to help the survivors aboard, after which we did our best to make them comfortable and attend to their injuries. There were Americans all over the 'Beagle' including the mess decks making life particularly chaotic but we coped, as people did during the war. We sank the blazing LST by gunfire and, at 8am,. proceeded back to Portsmouth at a speed of 33 knots to land survivors – it's a wonder that we survived! We arrived alongside at 11am. and passed our American friends into the welcoming arms of doctors and nurses etc.

The picture (over page) is a drawing by William Mcdowell which he did for the Illustrated London News at the time, and it captures the moment dramatically. The caption used by the magazine was as follows, '— INSIDE AN ENEMY MINEFIELD OFF THE CHERBOURG PENINSULA. The destroyer 'Beagle' saves the lives of American soldiers from a tank landing craft.' A well-worded

Drawing of the Beagle by William Mcdowell.

description follows. This incident was one of 'the most courageous and cold-blooded rescue ventures' that one war correspondent had ever seen at sea. American landing craft were going in to the beaches when one of them was hit by a shell. The British destroyer's searchlights were switched on, illuminating the struggling American soldiers in the water. The blazing hulk of the landing craft made the destroyer an easy target. Men swarmed down the ladders, plunging waist-deep into the sea hauling out the soldiers, some of them required six or seven men to pull them out, so sodden were their battle kit and life-jackets.

The destroyer which thus braved both mines and the enemy coastal batteries is one of a very successful pre-war type, built in 1930. The class exceeded the design speed with ease, and proved to be most economical of fuel. 'Beagle' is armed with four 4.7 in. guns and a number of smaller weapons for anti-aircraft purposes. She has four torpedo-tubes and a speed of 35 knots. (The picture and the accompanying description has been integrated into the Diary text by kind permission of the Illustrated London Weekly.)

It is only in retrospect that one starts to consider how dangerous the situation had been and perhaps experience some of the feelings that were sublimated at the time. An entry in the Diary recounts a visit to the AMMO ship at 4pm. in order to replenish 'Beagle's' ammunition, shells, depth charges etc. We anchored in the Solent at 5.30pm. At 8.30am. the following day we moved back to Portland again, arriving at 11am. and, with the Motor Boat lowered, I was Duty Coxswain during the afternoon.

```
          PUBLIC RECORD OFFICE          1  2  3  4  5  6
Reference:
      A O M  1 9 9 / 2 2 9 5                  1           2
      COPYRIGHT - NOT TO BE REPRODUCED PHOTOGRAPHICALLY WITHOUT PERMISSION
```

MOST SECRET

War Diary

9.6.1944
Friday

HOME COMMANDS

Operation "Neptune"

Mining

My 091547B and 091609B. Postponed 24 hours.
(C. in C. Portsmouth, 091824B to N.C.E.T.F.,
M.T.B.F.64)

Enemy Action

Convoy attacked. Two L.S.T. craft sunk.	Radar contact position 308 deg. Pointe de Barfleur 4.5 (?Am investigating 4 unknown vessels - speed nil.). (A/C. G.F.1, 090011 to Portsmouth)
	My 0011. 8 E-Boats course 280 degs. (A/C. G.F.1, 090018 to Portsmouth)
	Position 040 degs. Pointe de Barfleur 2 miles, course 155 degs. speed 35 knots. (A/C G.F.1, ?090021 to Portsmouth)
	Position of enemy 145 Pointe de Barfleur 5 course 145 degs. speed 10 knots. Contact lost. Am returning to patrol position. (A/C. G.F.1, 090050 to Portsmouth P.W.)
	Enemy position 063 Pointe de Barfleur 10 speed nil. (A/C G.F.1, 090113 to Portsmouth P.W.)
	?2 E-Boat. 2 L.S.T's torpedoed 049 degs. 48° N. 000 degs. 52° W. (BEAGLE, 090242 to S.O. Force "O")
	My 0242. E-boats driven off, Am picking up survivors. (BEAGLE, 090345 to S.O. Force "O")
	Have large number survivors on board. Rescue work proceeding. Where shall I make for on completion. (BEAGLE, 090500 to Portsmouth P.W.G.)
	E.T.A. 0945. Survivors 150, 12 dead will be buried at sea, 27 injured require treatment, 5 stretcher cases. (BEAGLE, 090804 to C. in C. Portsmouth)
L.C.T.(4) 608 damaged.	L.C.T.(4) 608 reports that during outward passage night of 7/8 June he was engaged by E-Boats and torpedoed forward and extensively damaged but sufficiently seaworthy to return U.K. Load which was R.A.F. regiment stores was transferred to M.T.2 (Capt. M/S.090041B to N.C.E.T.F.A.)

Enemy /...

Signal relating to Operation 'Neptune'.

We went alongside the jetty for 'coaling' purposes and this was supervised by 'Jimmy'(the naval term for the First Lieutenant) and completed by midnight.

At 2pm. on Sunday we went to anchor and shore leave was granted at 4.20pm. enabling us to land at Weymouth, a pleasant seaside resort, where I had supper. After the meal I visited a Methodist Church, the purpose of which I cannot recall, although it may have been to give thanks for surviving all the horrendous experiences that the 'Beagle' crew had suffered over the last twelve months? Prior to strolling around Weymouth I drank a couple of pints of cider, arriving back on board at about 10pm. The M.B. was hoisted at 11pm. and, after a night's sleep, we put to sea at 3am. on Monday, 12th.June with a convoy of 15 LST's. We were bombed, I think it was just one bomb, and we dropped depth charges suspecting that W(?) Boats were about – I think these were small German submarines. Arriving at Omaha Beach at 5pm. we left again at 9pm. to catch up with an empty convoy returning to Portland, arriving at

THE EVENING NEWS, TUESDAY, JULY 4, 19**-[?]

H.M.S. BEAGLE IN RESCUE DRAMA

(From Desmond Tighe, Reuter's correspondent aboard H.M.S. Beagle, in English Channel)

STEAMING inside an enemy minefield off the peninsula of Cherbourg, a British destroyer, H.M.S. Beagle, Lieut.-Comdr. Norman Murch, R.N., saved the lives of some American soldiers from a blazing tank landing craft.

It was the most courageous and cold-blooded rescue venture I have seen at sea.

It was 2 a.m., with rain falling, when the craft was struck, and as we began rescue work the destroyer's searchlights were deliberately switched on, illuminating the grey waters and the struggling figures. The blazing hulk of the landing craft made us stand out an easy target.

The bravery of the Beagle's officers and ship's company was something I shall never forget.

Bitterly Cold

It was bitterly cold, but men swarmed down the ladders, plunging waist deep into the sea to haul out soldiers.

A young sub-lieut. manned the whaler and pulled away into the night in search of other survivors. The ship's doctor—a London university man—immediately volunteered to go with him.

The captain stood high on the bridge shouting through the loudspeaker "Swim to the ship lads if you can. We will beat the — yet."

The coxswain, torpedo gunner's mate, stoker, petty officer, and two able seamen trying to save as many as possible jumped into the sea.

Narrow Escape

We picked them all up later. The torpedo gunner's mate narrowly missed being cut to pieces by the Beagle's propellors when he went over the stern to pull one man out.

When dawn came the wreck had drifted miles inside the German minefields, and was lying only a few miles off the peninsula of Cherbourg. Only then did the captain give up rescue work. We could find no more survivors.

The blazing hulk was sunk by gunfire and we steamed for home.

Newspaper clipping from the Evening News reporting on Beagle's courageous rescue.

8am. on Tuesday, on which day I was again the Duty Coxswain during the morning The early part of the morning was rough and windy and this can make things rathe tricky for our fairly small Motor Boat, but the weather calmed down toward lunchtime. The M.B. made one trip ashore and was then hoisted at 2pm. after which we moved to Portsmouth and anchored at 5pm. We proceeded to sea on anti submarine patrol at 8pm. accompanied by the destroyers 'Venus, Scourge an Alconquin', adopting a 'Two-watch' system as we had done before (very tiring) and during the night, dropped more depth charges with no obvious result. Back a Portland, we left the ship's Postman, the Canteen Manager and two stewards ashore On Wednesday at 4pm. we were on patrol again, sailing to France with a convoy o

8 merchantmen, accompanied by HMS Scourge and arriving at 5.30pm. We left two hours later, resuming patrol duties again at 11pm. again with the ship's crew divided into two 'Watches'. We were beginning to feel 'chokka'! The patrol lasted through the forenoon of Thursday but then we had to return to Portsmouth at 11am. for repairs, arriving at 1pm. The defect took 36 hours to repair and consisted of making good the Motor Boat's damaged screw, the boat having been run aground by the *other* coxswain – but then I would say that wouldn't I? Shore leave was granted. On Friday, 16th.June we went to anchor and shore leave was again granted but the liberty boat was not available until 3pm. for what reason I cannot remember and, although leave was granted until 9pm. we had to wait until 11.30pm. for the transport back aboard. There is a note in the Diary that suggests I had thoughts of going home but, bearing in mind the consequences, it must have been only a fleeting thought? I went to the cinema in Southsea, just along the coast from Portsmouth, and saw the film 'Tender Comrade', with Ginger Rogers, and this was coupled with another film entitled 'Tornado' about which I can remember nothing! At 9.30am. on Saturday we went alongside the AMMO ship again, moving to the oiler at 1pm. and anchoring at 5pm. On Sunday I went ashore to collect the repaired Motor Boat promised for 9am. but, after messing about waiting for it until midday, I returned to the 'Beagle', the boat having then been promised for 6pm. I went ashore in the whaler (under sail) to Southsea Pier, reaching there at 3pm. and, after a meal at the 'Savoy', continued to the Odeon cinema to see 'On Approval' and 'Frontier Badman', films that I had not seen before. After the cinema, I made another attempt to collect the Motor Boat, it now being 8pm. but it was still not ready! I had supper and eventually arrived back at the 'Beagle', plus Motor Boat and liberty men at a quarter past midnight on Monday. During the next four days we were on continuous patrol and on this occasion we were not allowed to sling our hammocks, I cannot think why? It was very rough and windy and we were on the monstrous two-watch system again.

On Thursday the sea calmed and, in place of the rough weather, we enjoyed lovely sunshine and a flat sea. The serenity was spoiled at 11pm. by 'Beagle' being attacked by six German aircraft, but we damaged some with gunfire also managing to dodge yet another 'tin fish' (torpedo). The machine gun attack by the aircraft lasted no more than fifteen minutes, but it was frightening while it lasted. We resumed patrol at 3am. on Friday, 23rd.June 1944 and investigated a Radar contact near the French coast, discovering an unoccupied large craft which we sank with gunfire. At 6.30am. we picked up some Germans from the water.........

This is how my Diary ends and not long afterwards I left HMS Beagle to join an Aircraft Carrier, HMS Arbiter, via a short stay in Portsmouth barracks, HMS Victory, to spend a year in the Far East, but that is another story.

It is worth including the activities of HMS 'Beagle' from the time of my departure to her demise eighteen months or so later. She continued in Operation 'Neptune' until July 1944, with Channel patrols and the escorting of landing craft and ships between England and France. After two periods of repairs towards the end of 1944, 'Beagle' was sidelined prior to rejoining the 8th. Escort Group. She was reallocated to Plymouth early in 1945, taking part in escort duties in the Western Channel before sharing the responsibility, with HMS Bulldog, of accepting the surrender of the German garrison, based in the Channel Islands, on 9th. May 1945. 'Beagle' spent some time in the Category 'C' Reserve at Devonport, HMS Drake, finally being approved for scrapping on 22nd.December 1945. A month later she was handed over to BISCO at Rosyth, moving to the Metal Industries shipbreaking yard two days later. So ended the last of the illustrious 'Beagles', their history stretching back into the distant past.

LETTERS TO THE EDITOR

The Navy's key D-Day role

SIR — Is the Royal Navy once again being deliberately forgotten? So far, publicity for the celebrations to mark the 50th anniversary of the Normandy landings has been dominated by controversies over accommodation and sanitary arrangements ashore (report, April 14).

There has not yet been sufficiently clear recognition of the Navy's key role in the events of 50 years ago. Operation Neptune, the maritime component of Overlord and the most complex naval operation ever conceived, was planned by a predominantly British team under the inspired leadership of Admiral Sir Bertram Ramsay.

It was then executed by a fleet most of which flew the white ensign. Even on the American beaches the British effort was considerable. At Omaha, for example, three-quarters of the minesweepers were British, and there were more British infantry landing ships than American. At Utah, a Royal Navy monitor and three cruisers made up half the heavy bombardment force.

The promised presence this June of the American carrier George Washington, welcome though it is, may give a misleading impression of an American-dominated operation. There were no American carriers anywhere near Normandy in June, 1944, for Neptune did not top the US Navy's list of priorities. On the very day the landings took place, the main American fleet, the mightiest carrier force the world had ever seen, sailed from its anchorage at Majuro in the Pacific to score a crushing victory over the Japanese in the Philippine Sea.

The US Navy was more than happy to leave Europe to the US Army, the British and the Canadians while it avenged Pearl Harbour.

Neptune was thus the last time that the Royal Navy, ably supported by the Merchant Navy and the Royal Canadian Navy, took the lead in a decisive maritime operation against a great power.

One hopes that there are no ulterior motives in the apparently rather muted expressions of this fact. Or are there elements within the Ministry of Defence trying to play it down lest it strengthen the arguments for maintaining British amphibious capabilities?

Indeed, what better way of marking the anniversary of the greatest amphibious operation of all than by ordering at last the two long-promised amphibious transport docks (LPDs) the modern successors of that British armada of 50 years ago?

ERIC GROVE
London SW13

58

AFTERTHOUGHTS – 60 YEARS LATER

I can still recall, albeit vaguely, the feelings of anxiety that I experienced during 'Beagle's' trips to North Russia during mountainous seas, high winds, ice and snow and extreme cold, particularly those going in a northerly direction. As I endeavour to think back, the relief that we all felt in making port, either in Russia or in the UK, was palpable. It seemed remarkable to me that the designers of warships such as the 'Beagle' were able to calculate the balance between seaworthiness (length and breadth of the hull, thickness and strength of the metal) and maximum firepower in the form of guns, depth charges, torpedoes etc., to say nothing of designing all the equipment necessary to provide power for propulsion, heat, light etc. Only those who have experienced nature at its worst, miles from anywhere, together with the thought that, should disaster strike, the chance of being plucked from the icy waters was virtually nil, can appreciate the situation. As I said in the main part of the book, adrenaline took over in dangerous circumstances, redirecting the elements of anxiety, but it was when we were just involved in escorting the convoys on routine days that the vile conditions had their effect. The weight below the waterline had to balance the weight above to ensure that in the event of 'rolling' 'Beagle' would always be able to right itself. There are numerous records of ships 'turning turtle'! It was almost impossible to sleep during the periods of rough weather, and I can remember how much more difficult it was to concentrate on the green Radar screen to watch for 'blips' indicating an object (the enemy?) whilst suffering from sleep deprivation.

Warships such as the 'Beagle' operated a two-watch system, the whole ship's company being divided into two equal groups and, for convenience, labelled 'Starboard' and 'Port', yours truly having charge of the 'Starboard Watch'. Each 'Watch' was responsible for the smooth running of the ship when on duty, and a two-watch system functioned during 'Action Stations' as mentioned in the Diary. However, it would be humanly impossible for individuals to alternate between four hours on watch and four hours off watch and so it was necessary therefore to make another division of the ship's company into three groups, thus making it possible, whilst at sea, to operate a three-watch system, allowing for four hours on duty and eight hours off duty. If the twenty four hour day was split into four-hour watches, it doesn't require a maths degree to see that each of the three groups would be on duty at the same time each day and, because some four watches are more arduous than some, it would have been most unfair. Hence the reason for the 'Dog Watches', the period between 4pm. and 8pm. being divided into two two-hour sessions (1600-1800 and 1800-2000) causing a rotation of the watch periods. In the Diary I mentioned 'Jock' Miller, a typical Scot and a particular friend, who was in charge of the 'Port Watch'. He was slightly older than me and was married – I had no female attachments – and during one period of leave when he was 'On Watch' and I was free to go ashore, I stayed with 'Jocks' wife for a few days at his invitation and with his wife's full agreement. Their house was in Glasgow and it was like home from home, with all the comforts that one would enjoy at one's own home. It was a reflection of society at that time that no-one even considering the possibility impropriety or what people might think or say. Things like morals, loyalty, respectability, consideration for each other, honesty were taken for granted in the world that 'Jock' and I inhabited, unlike the present day, with the evils exacerbated by the 'Tabloids' and Television. Life and Society have changed over the last sixty years and not always for the better.

THE LAST WORD

I think it is fair to say that, in the opinion of some experts, the progress of World War II would have been dramatically changed, had war equipment etc., not been supplied to Russia via the North Atlantic Convoys, arguing that the British and American supplies were an important factor in Russia's defeat of the Germans on the Eastern Front. The German armoured divisions that were needed to be committed to try to stem the Russian onslaught were thus unable to be moved to France to increase the German defences etc., and Operation 'Overlord' might have turned out differently.

Footnotes

1. There is a very good account of the early days of Operation 'Overlord' in the 'D' Day 50th. Anniversary Commemorative Official Souvenir Prospectus of Events entitled 'The Role of the Naval Forces'.

2. RADAR stands for Radio Angle Detection and Ranging, and was developed during the 1930's. An explanation of its operation can be found earlier in the book. An ECHO SOUNDER functioned in a similar way, the sound wave being sent downwards to the sea- bed from which it was reflected, thus indicating the depth. SONAR, working on a similar principal, with the sound wave beamed horizontally beneath sea surface, was ideal for spotting submarines.

3. *Supplies to Russia*: To put things into context and using the PQ 18 as a reasonably typical convoy, the 39 ships which sailed carried 4,400 vehicles, 835 tanks, 566 aircraft, over 11,000 tons of high explosives, over 157,000 tons of general cargo and 9,541 tons of fuel oil (not including that carried by the escort oilers). Over the period of four years between 70 and 80 convoys went to or from Russia.

POSTSCRIPT

WAR, MUSIC AND THE SEA

Classical music has always been a large part of my life and I was fortunate that I did not completely lose touch with it during my service on HMS Beagle, as readers will have observed.

Music has many faces and captures and exposes many emotions, just like the sea, serenity, excitement, sadness, anger etc., emotions that are heightened during wartime.

Readers will have noticed that the West African waters were more conducive to listening to music than those of the North Atlantic, the record playing equipment preferring the calm seas of the former.

Many people are unaware of the power of music (we are left in no doubt of the might of the oceans) although recent research seems to provide evidence of the tangible effects of listening to music, particularly Mozart, on the individual.

It is interesting to note that 'War Films' such as the 'Cruel Sea', have their emotional impact intensified by background music, either composed specially or chosen from various sources. Another prime example of the power of music was the use of the opening four notes of Beethoven's Fifth Symphony, translated into Morse Code to sound the letter 'V' for victory, instrumental in psychologically undermining the confidence of the Hun.

Music has always had a power for good or ill and one of many obvious examples of it being used to add impetus to an attack, was the 'skirl of the pipes' that accompanied the Scots as they went into battle!

Music can be and in fact was a morale booster during the time of war and a spur to action during both the World Wars and, during the Second World War, it included Classical Concerts, E.N.S.A. (Entertainments National Service Association) many of the contributors going on to become household names after the war, singing popular wartime songs, Vera Lynne etc.etc.

Peter Ward

APPENDICES

The following appendices list the merchantmen that sailed in the convoys to and from Russia during the period June 1943 and June 1944 whilst HMS Beagle was on escort duty and I was a member of the crew.

There are also lists of the Royal Navy ships involved in escort duty during the sailing of these convoys, some for the whole trip, either to or from Russia, and some for part of the time due to the need for refuelling, the result of damage, other duties etc.

A large number of merchant ships were built in America during the Second World War, many called 'Liberty Ships' for obvious reasons, and they were instrumental in keeping Britain 'alive' at a critical time in the war, sailing to and from America with food and equipment.

Ships constructed in the USA were often crewed by Americans and, as well as coping with U-boats and the possibility of attack from German Warships between Britain and America, they were also used for convoys to Northern Russia, commonly called 'Russian Convoys'. Vital supplies were fed to Russia through Murmansk etc.

A great many merchantmen were sunk prior to the introduction of the Convoy System, and although convoys with naval escorts reduced the number of sinkings, it wasn't until the introduction of Escort Carriers, with their 'eyes in the sky' (aircraft such as the Swordfish) which could locate German submarines more easily than surface craft, that the battle against U-boats turned in favour of the Allies.

'Beagle', of course, shared the sinking of 'U355' with the aircraft from the escort carrier HMS Tracker.

APPENDIX A - CONVOY JW54B

Merchant Navy:

Royal Navy Escorts:

Merchantmen:	*Destroyers:*	*Minesweepers:*
Arthur L. Perry	Ashanti	Halcyon
Daldorch	Beagle	Speedwell
Empire Lionel	Hardy	
Empire Stalwart	Matchless	*Corvettes:*
Eugene Field	Middleton	
Fort Columbia	Muskateer	Dianella
Fort McMurray	Obdurate	Poppy
Fort Poplar	Saladin	Rhododendron
Horace Gray	Saumarez	
John Fitch	Savage	*Cruisers:*
Ocean Strength	Scourge	
Rathlin	Skate	Bermuda
San Adolfo (Escort oiler)	Venus	Jamaica
Thomas Kearns	Vigilant	Kent
William L. Marcy		

This convoy arrived at Archangel having avoided detection and attack during its passage from Loch Ewe.

The Commodore was aboard DALDORCH.

APPENDIX B - CONVOY RA55A

Merchant Navy: **Royal Navy Escorts:**

Merchantmen: *Destroyers:*   *Minesweepers:*

Arthur L.Perry   Ashanti   Hound
Daniel Drake   Athabascan   Hydra
Edmund Fanning   Beagle   Seagull
Empire Carpenter   Matchless
Empire Celia   Meteor   *Corvettes:*
Empire Nigel   Milne
Fort McMurray   Muskateer   Acanthus
Fort Yukon   Opportune   Borage
Gilbert Stuart   Savage   Dianella
Henry Villard   Saumarez   Poppy
James Smith   Scorpion   Wallflower
Junecrest   Stord
Mijdrecht   Virago   *Cruisers:*
Ocean Strength   Westcott
Ocean Vanity   Belfast
Ocean Verity   Jamaica
Park Holland   Norfolk
Rathlin   Sheffield
San Adolfo (Escort oiler)
Thomas Kearns   *Battleship:*
Thomas Sim Lee
William L. Marcy   Duke of York.
William Windom

This convoy reached Loch Ewe without loss and with no enemy contact.

The Commodore was aboard FORT YUKON.

APPENDIX C - CONVOY JW57

Merchant Navy:

Royal Navy Escorts:

Merchantmen:	*Destroyers:*	*Minesweepers:*
Alexander White	Beagle	Hydra
British Valour (Escort oiler)	Boadicea	Loyalty
Byron Darnton	Impulsive	Orestes
Caesar Rodney	Keppel	Rattlesnake
Charles Bulfinch	Matchless	
Charles M. Schwab	Meteor	*Corvettes:*
Copeland	Milne	
Daphnella	Obedient	Bluebell
Edward Sparrow	Offa	Burdock
Empire Carpenter	Onslaught	Camelia
Empire Celia	Oribi	Dianella
Empire Nigel	Savage	Lotus
Fort Brule	Serapis	Rhododendron
Fort McMurray	Swift	
Fort Romaine	Verulam	*Cruisers:*
Henry H. Brown	Vigilant	
Henry Lomb	Walker	Black Prince
Jefferson Davis	Wanderer	Berwick
John A. Donald	Watchman	Jamaica
John A. Quitman		
John Langdon	*Aircraft Carrier:*	*Frigates:*
John Rutledge		
John Sharp Williams	Chaser	Byron
John Stevenson		Strule
John Powell		
John Woolman		
Joshua W. Alexander		
Lord Delaware		
Louis D. Brandeis		
Lucerna		
Maria M. Meloney		
Mijdrecht		

Merchant Navy contin...

Merchantmen:

Nathan Towson
Nathaniel Alexander
Ocean Strength
Philip F. Thomas
Richard M. Johnson
Robert Eden
Robert J. Collier
San Ambrosio (Escort oiler)
Stevenson Taylor, H.
Thomas Hartley
William H. Webb

Although there was contact with the enemy, and U-boats sank their first and only Royal Navy Escort vessel HMS Mahratta (there were only 17 survivors), no merchant ships were sunk.

The Commodore was aboard FORT ROMAINE.

APPENDIX D - CONVOY RA 57

Merchant Navy: **Royal Navy Escorts:**

Merchantmen: *Destroyers:*   *Minesweepers:*

Abner Nash	Beagle	Gleaner
Aert Van Der Neer	Boadicea	Hydra
Albert C. Ritchie	Impulsive	Loyalty
Bernard N. Baker	Keppel	Onyx
Charles A. McAllister	Matchless	Orestes
Charles Scribner	Meteor	Ready
Copeland	Milne	Seagull
Edward L. Grant	Obedient	
Edwin L. Drake	Offa	*Corvettes:*
Empire Bard	Onslaught	
Empire Pickwick	Orbi	Bluebell
Empire Ploughman	Savage	Camellia
Empire Tourist	Serapis	Lotus
Fort Crevecoeur	Swift	Rhododendron
Fort Norfolk	Verulam	
Fort Slave	Vigilant	*Cruisers:*
Henry Bacon		
Henry Wynkoop	*Aircraft Carrier:*	Black Prince:
John H. B. Latrobe		
John La Farge	Chaser	
Paul Hamilton Hayne		
Philip Livingston		
Richard H. Alvey		
Robert Lowry		
Samuel McIntyre		
San Adolf (Escort oiler)		
San Ambrosio (Escort oiler)		
San Cirilo. (Escort oiler)		
Thorstein Veblen		
Willard Hall		
William Tyler Page		
Winfred L. Smith		
Woodbridge N. Ferris		

U-boats were sunk and damaged, mainly by Swordfish aircraft from 'Chaser'. The new approach adopted earlier proved to be very effective. Aircraft were better able o spot U-boats than surface craft, and could damage and sink them. The use of an aircraft carrier to accompany a convoy, starting with JW57, was a major blow to Hitler's submarine strategy, and was instrumental in saving many lives.

The Commodore was aboard FORT CREVECOEUR.

APPENDIX E - CONVOY JW58

Merchant Navy:

Royal Navy Escorts:

Merchantmen:	*Destroyers:*	*Minesweepers:*
Andrew Carnegie	Beagle	Onyx
Arunah S. Abell	Boadicea	Orestes
Barbara Frietchie	Keppel	Rattlesnake
Benjamin H. Latrobe	Impulsive	
Benjamin Schlesinger	Inconstant	*Corvettes:*
Charles Gordon Curtis	Obedient	
Charles Henderson	Offa	Bluebell
Dolabella	Onslow	Honeysuckle
Edward P. Alexander	Opportune	Lotus
Eloy Alfaro	Oribi	
Empire Prowess	Orwell	*Sloops:*
Fort Columbia	Saumarez	
Fort Hall	Serapis	Magpie
Fort Kullyspell	Scorpion	Starling
Fort Vercheres	Stord	Wild Goose
Fort Yukon	Venus	Wren
Francis Scott Key	Westcott	Whimbrels
Francis Vigo	Whitehall	
George Gale	Wrestler	*Cruisers:*
Gilbert Stuart		
George M. Cohan	*Aircraft Carriers:*	Diadem.
George T. Angell		Milwaukee
Grace Abbott	Activity.	
Hawkins Fudske	Tracker.	
Henry Villard		
James Smith		
John B. Lennon		
John Carver		
John Davenport		
John McDonogh		
John T. Holt		
Joseph N. Nocollet		
Joshua Thomas		

Merchant Navy contin...

Merchantmen:

Joyce Kilmer
Julien Poydras
Lacklan
Morris Hillquit
Nicholas Biddle
Noreg
Pierre S. Dupont
Rathlin
Thomas Sim Lee
Townsend Harris
W.R. Grace
William D. Byron
William Matson
William McKinley
William Moultrie
William Pepper
William S. Thayer

Considerable air and U-boat activity dogged this convoy. Included in the list of destroyers are the names of the 2nd. Escort Group, under the famous Captain F. J. Walker. Russian destroyers were also present for a short time in the North Russian waters. The American Cruiser Milwaukee was to be handed over to the Russian Northern Fleet. 'Beagle' and 'Tracker's' aircraft sank the German U-boat, U 355.

APPENDIX F - CONVOY RA58

Merchant Navy:

Merchantmen:

Alexander White.
British Valour (Escort oiler)
Byron Darnton
Caesar Rodney
Charles Bulfinch
Charles M. Schwab
Copeland
Daphnella
Edward Sparrow
Empire Celia
Fort McMurray
Fort Romaine
Henry B. Brown
Henry Lomb
Jefferson Davis
John A. Donald
John A. Quitman
John Rutledge
John Sharp
John Stevenson
John W. Powell
John Woolman
Joshua W. Alexander
Lord Delaware
Louis D. Brandeis
Lucerna
Marie M. Meloney
Mijdrecht
Nathan Towson
Nathaniel Alexander
Ocean Strength
Philip F. Thomas
Rathlin

Royal Navy Escorts:

Destroyers:

Beagle
Boadicea
Impulsive
Inconstant
Keppel
Obedient
Offa.
Onslow
Opportune
Oribi
Orwell
Saumarez
Scorpion
Serapis
Stord
Walker
Westcott
Whitehall
Wrestler

Aircraft Carriers:

Activity
Tracker

Corvettes:

Bluebell
Honeysuckle

Sloops:

Starling
Magpie
Whimbrel
Wild Goose
Wren.

Cruisers:

Diadem

Merchant Navy contin...

Merchantmen:

Richard M. Johnson
Robert J. Collier
Stevenson Taylor
Thomas Hartley
William H. Webb

Operation 'Tungsten' (damage to the 'Tirpitz' by aircraft) eradicated the need for distant cover needed for Convoy JW57, i.e. the forces involved with the 'Tirpitz'.

U-boat interception of this convoy was thwarted and German 'subs' failed to make contact, thus ensuring that Convoy JW58 arrived safely at Loch Ewe.

The Commodore was aboard FORT ROMAINE.

APPENDIX G

A special group of Escort ships was despatched, at speed, to Kola Inlet to collec
ships and the crew of USS Milwaukee etc. The personnel ship Nea Hellas developec
defects and had to return to the UK, leaving American and Russian personnel to be
distributed among the other ships. Operation 'Overlord' was, obviously, on the nea
horizon and this precluded the running of JW convoys (convoys to Russia) in orde
that all the Royal Navy resources could be concentrated on the critical preparatior
necessary for 'D' Day.

Destroyers:	Frigates:	Cruisers:	Aircraft Carriers:
Beagle	Cape Breton	Diadem	Activity
Boadicea	Grou		Fencer
Inconstant	Outremont		
Westcott	Waskesiu		
Whitehall			
Wrestler			

APPENDIX H - CONVOY RA59

Merchant Navy:

Royal Navy Escorts:

Merchantmen:

Andrew Carnegie
Arunah S. Abell
Charles Henderson
Dolabella
Edward P. Alexander
Fort Brule
Fort Columbia
Fort Hall
Fort Kullyspell
Fort Yukon
Francis Scott Key
Francis Vigo
George Gale
George M. Cohan
George T. Angell
Gilbert Stuart
Grace Abott
Hawkins Fudske
Henry Villard
James Smith
John B. Lennon
John Carver
John Davenport
John McDonogh
John T. Holt
John N. Nocollet
Joshua Thomas
Joyce Kilmer.
Julien Poydras.
Lapland.
Morris Hillquit.
Nicholas Biddle.
Noreg.(Escort oiler)

Destroyers:

Beagle
Boadicea
Inconstant
Keppel
Marne
Matchless
Meteor
Milne
Muskateer
Ulysses
Verulum
Virago
Walker
Whitehall

Aircraft Carriers:

Activity
Fencer

Corvettes:

Lotus

Cruisers:

Diadem

Frigates:

Cape Breton
Grou
Outremont
Waskesiu

2 Russian destroyers joined the convoy in North Russian waters, plus a number of smaller vessels.

Merchant Navy contin...

Merchantmen:

Pierre S. Dupont
Robert Eden
Thomas Sim Lee
Townsend Harris
William D. Byron
William Matson
William McKinley
William Moultrie
William Pepper
William S. Thayer

Atrocious weather conditions made carrier aircraft operations very hazardous especially with the flight decks covered by as much as six inches of snow at times William S. Thayer was sunk with the loss of 43 of her crew and passengers. 19? were picked up, mainly by the destroyer Whitehall. At one time a line of 1? 'U' boats was patrolling off the Coast of Bear Island. 'Fencer's' swordfish sank ? 'U' boats, and enabled the convoy to continue unmolested, and to dock safely, par? of it at Loch Ewe and the rest at the Clyde.

The Commodore was aboard FORT YUKON.

APPENDIX I

U 355 (I have tried to keep the 'added' information in balance with the Diary as a whole so that the Diary retains its integrity, but I feel that the appendices etc., are worth including.)

In correspondence with Lieutenant Commander Colin McMillan, the author of the 'foreword' to this book, the subject of the sinking of U 355 arose. There is no mention of the sinking in my Diary, I feel some detail is worth quoting as an appendix.

Colin very kindly sent me documents including official ones, some of which talk of uncorroborated evidence used to confirm the sinking, together with questions about the actual date. As I mentioned earlier, the Diary does not record the sinking of a U-boat at this time, although it does record considerable surface U-boat and convoy escort activity. It also records the rescue of the pilot involved in the demise of U 355, without going into detail. I have reread the appropriate passages in books listed in the bibliography where there is reference to the sinking of U 355, all of which link 'Beagle' and aircraft from 'Tracker' with the sinking. ('Beagle's' logbook is missing.)

Richard Woodman refers to the shooting down of a German aircraft BV 138 which, incidentally is noted in my Diary, and also the attack on the U-boat by an Avenger from 'Tracker'. He also suggests that enough damage was done to the submarine to enable 'Beagle' (Captain, Lieutenant Commander Murch) to administer the *coupe de grace*. My Diary mentions an aircraft crashing into the rear of 'Tracker' whilst trying to land and Woodman includes a gory account of this episode, naming the pilot as Sub-lieutenant Ballantyne. In the book I also mention the rescuing of an airman and, using Woodman as the source, I can name him as Lieutenant Lucey. He was, incidentally, the pilot of a 'Wildcat' aircraft from 'Tracker' and it was reported that, having attempted an attack on U 355 and failed because of faulty mechanism involving the dropping of depth charges, he angrily made a beeline for the sub's conning tower, causing him to crash, later to be picked up by 'Beagle'. It was said that he later denied this, but Colin puts this down to official pressure concerned with the loss of an aircraft. To quote from Colin's letter: 'The extraordinary thing about this story is that Donald Lucey's amazing courage in attacking U 355 was never properly recognised because someone in 'Tracker' decided that they could not report that he had virtually written off his 'Wildcat' in actually flying into the conning tower and periscope. One 'Wildcat' fighter seemed fair exchange for one U-boat! The day after when Lucey had recovered from his frozen state in his dinghy, covered with glace icing when we found him after one and a half hours, he told me that when he saw the attacking 'Avenger's' depth charges did not fall from the bomb racks, he was so bloody angry that he flew his fighter straight at the U-boat.' Colin adds in a postscript that he recently heard the explanation for the 'Avenger's' problem. They were built in the USA, the Depth charges were British and did not mate properly with the US release mechanism. Colin also refers to the date of the sinking, indicating that he is uncertain as to whether it was 1st. or 2nd.April but, on balance, thinks it was the 1st.April 1944 (My inclination is to rely on the reports of those who took part, such as Colin.)

Ruegg and Hague include in their description of the activities of the Russian bound Convoy JW58 which, incidentally, lists all the merchant ships and Naval escorts, a brief mention of U 355, linking 'Beagle' and 'Tracker' to its sinking, albeit giving the date as 31st.March 1944.

John English gives a history of 'Beagles' activities from its launch in 1930 to its demise in 1946. He refers to Convoy JW58 and 'Beagle's' participation in the sinking of U 355 with aircraft from the escort carrier 'Tracker', quoting the date as 1st.April 1994.

APPENDIX J

The following are the British and Allied Warships lost during Arctic Convoy Operations. The destroyer 'Mahratta' was the only one lost during the year that I served on the 'Beagle'.

Cruisers: Edinburgh, Trinidad.

Destroyers: Achates, Hardy, Mahratta, Matabele, Punjabi, Sokrushitelny, Somali.

Sloops: Kite, Lark, Lapwing.

Frigates: Goodall.

Corvettes: Bluebell, Denbigh Castle, Tunsberg Castle.

Minesweepers: Bramble, Gossamer, Leda, Niger.

Submarines: P 551 (Jastrzab) Sunk in error.

Armed Whalers: Shera, Sulla.

31 German submarines were sunk during the Arctic Operations.
The 'Scharnhorst' was sunk – detail in the diary.
3 destroyers and 2 Auxiliary vessels/escort were also sunk.

PETER WARD -
ROYAL NAVAL SERVICE SHEET FOR WORLD WAR II
1941/1946

Shore Establishments & Ships served on	*Rating*	*Period of service*
Glendower (N.Wales)	Ordinary Seaman	4th Oct, 1941 - 19th Nov, 1941
Victory (Isle of Man)	ditto	20th Nov, 1941 - 18th Dec, 194?
Victory (HMS Sweet Briar)	ditto	19th Dec, 1941 - 24th Apr, 1942
Pembroke	ditto	24th Apr, 1942 - 25th Apr, 1942
Badger (Sunk Head Fort)	ditto	25th Apr, 1942 - 1st Dec, 1942
Badger (Sunk Head Fort)	ditto	2nd Dec, 1942 - 14th Apr, 1943
Mercury	Able Seaman	15th Apr, 1943 - 16th Apr, 1943
King Alfred (CW Candidate)	ditto	17th Apr, 1943 - 1st May, 1943
Mercury	ditto	2nd May, 1943 - 10th May, 194?
Drake 1V (RDF)	ditto	11th May, 1943 - 2nd June, 194.
Orlando (HMS Beagle)	ditto	3rd June, 1943 - 17th Jul, 1943
Philoctetes (HMS Beagle)	A/Leading Seaman (Radar) (Ty) confirmed 9th June, 1943	
Philoctetes (HMS Beagle)	ditto	18th Jul, 1943 - 13th Oct, 1943
Orlando (HMS Beagle)	ditto	14th Oct, 1943 - 29th Feb, 1944
Orlando (HMS Beagle)	R.P.(P)	1st Mar, 1944 - 3rd May, 1944
Orlando (HMS Beagle)	A/Leading Seaman (Radar)	4th May, 1944 – 30th Jul, 1944
	(Confirmed Leading Seaman (Ty) R.P.2 - 9th June, 1944)	
Drake	ditto	31st Jul, 1944 - 15th Sep, 1944
Heron	ditto	16th Sep, 1944 - 27th Oct, 1944
Valkyrie	ditto	28th Oct, 1944 - 10th Nov, 1944
Drake	ditto	17th Nov, 1944 - 5th Dec, 1944
HMS Arbiter	ditto	6th Dec, 1944 - 24th Jan, 1946
Drake	ditto	25th Jan, 1946 - 25th May, 1946

BIBLIOGRAPHY

The Arctic Convoys (1941-1945) by Richard Woodman.
Published by John Murray.

Convoys to Russia (1941-1945) by Bob Ruegg and Arnold Hague.
Published by the World Ship Society.

Amazon to Ivanhoe (British standard destroyers of the 1930's) by John English.
Published by the World Ship Society.

The Imperial War Museum – Photographic Archives (London).

The Public Records Office (Kew, London).

The Illustrated London News.

Newspaper cuttings at the time.

The Diary.

PETER WARD

BACKGROUND

Peter Ward is the author of a book entitled, 'From Africa to the Arctic'. The book is based on a Diary that he kept for a year whilst serving as a member of the crew of the Destroyer, HMS Beagle, involved in West African convoy duty, an escort for Russian Convoys and 'D' Day landing activities.

Peter Ward was born in 1922. Both his parents were musical and he was educated at Walpole Grammar School, Ealing, London, during which time he learned to play the piano and the violin. He has always been involved in the world of 'Classical Music'. After a period working for the Inland Revenue he joined the Royal Navy in September 1941. He qualified as a Radar operator in Douglas, Isle of Man and joined the crew of the Corvette, Sweet Briar to find himself based in

Iceland and involved in patrolling the North Atlantic in search of a German Battleship. Fortunately for him no contact was made! Following a year on a Fort off the East Coast on Sunk Head Sands, he joined the crew of HMS Beagle, a destroyer, keeping a daily diary for the whole of the period from June 1943 to June 1944. The Diary details 'Beagle's' activities escorting convoys up and down the coast of West Africa, acting as one of many escorts protecting convoys to North Russia and back, and finally describes the assault of the French Coast on 'D' Day in which HMS Beagle took part. The last year of the Second World War saw Peter as a crew member of HMS Arbiter, a merchantman converted to serve as an aircraft carrier, based at Sydney, Australia and serving the British Fleet off the Coast of Japan, during which time 'VE' and 'VJ' days were celebrated.

After the war, Peter trained as a teacher at University College, Worcester. He was also a student at the Birmingham School of Music, now the Birmingham Conservatoire, studying piano and violin. He took up a teaching post in Oxford, followed by a Deputy Headship, concluding his teaching career as a Senior Lecturer in Music at Summerfield College, Kidderminster and Shenstone/N.E.W. College Bromsgrove. Having already obtained three LRAM's in the early 1950's, he gained an Open University BA Honours Degree in the early 1980's. In 1980 he was jointly responsible with Louis Carus, the then Principal, in forming what is now the Birmingham Conservatoire Association. He was awarded an Honorary Fellowship by Birmingham Conservatoire in 1996 for services to music. With Joyce Messenger, he initiated and organised the Bromsgrove Festival Young Musicians' Platform for twelve years and was the accompanist for Barnt Green Choral Society for twelve years. He has been a Staff Tutor for the Orchestral Courses at Hawkwood College, Stroud for the past thirty years, as well as performing, teaching, adjucating and serving on numerous committees.

Peter has been married to Jean for over 52 years and they have two daughters, both professional musicians. He has appreciated her help and encouragement throughout the production of the book.

ACKNOWLEDGEMENTS

My thanks to Jean, my wife, for all her help and encouragement throughout the production of the book.

My thanks to Lieutenant Commander Colin McMillan for details of the trip to the Russian Destroyer and its aftermath (!) and the sinking of the U-boat 355 (Appendix K) etc.

My thanks to friends and relations for their encouragement.

CAVALIER TRUST

HMS Cavalier - The HMS Cavalier (Chatham) Trust Ltd

HMS Cavalier was one of 96 War Emergency destroyers ordered between 1940 and 1942. Built at Samuel White's Cowes yard, Cavalier was launched on 7th.April 1944, and was completed in November 1944 before joining the Home Fleet. During the early months of 1945 she undertook a number of operations off Norway and in the Arctic and was awarded the Battle Honour 'Arctic 1945'. By Spring 1945 Cavalier was operating in the Western Atlantic and after the war in Europe ended, she was allocated to the British Pacific Fleet, arriving at Colombo in time to take part in the final clearing up operation in the East Indies.

Refitted following the war HMS Cavalier returned to active service in 1957 as a unit of the 8th.Destroyer Squadron, Far East Fleet. She remained in service until 1972 when she paid off for the last time at Chatham at the end of an eventful 28 year career. In that time she had steamed 564,140 miles, seen action in the Second World War and completed many years of strenuous Cold War and peacekeeping duties.

In 1983 HMS Cavalier became a museum ship first at Southampton and then at Brighton. In December 1998, after a decade on the River Tyne (mostly closed to visitors), Cavalier was acquired by The HMS Cavalier (Chatham) Trust Ltd., established to preserve the ship at The Historic Dockyard, Chatham. The Trust is a registered charity and a subsidiary of Chatham Historic Dockyard Trust, the charitable organisation established by government in 1984 to take stewardship of the 80 acre Historic Dockyard following the closure of Chatham Dockyard.

In 1999 the generous support of the National Heritage Memorial Fund enabled a major programme of hull repairs to be undertaken to allow HMS Cavalier to be towed to her new berth at Chatham. Work to secure her long term preservation continues.

HMS Cavalier is now displayed in the largest of the Historic Dockyard's three dry docks as part of a major 'three ship attraction' with HMS Ocelot, an O class submarine, and HMS Gannet, a sloop of the Victorian Navy.

Among her many duties, she was one of the escorts for the homeward-bound Russian *Convoy RA64* and later operated in the Western Approaches undertaking duties which included the high speed escort of the liner-turned-troopships RMS Queen Mary and RMS Queen Elisabeth.

Her preservation by the HMS Cavalier Trust is a memorial to the 153 Royal Navy destroyers sunk during the Second World War, with the loss of nearly 30,000 men.

(Reproduced from the Trust's own literature)
Telephone: 01634 823800
(www.chdt.org.uk)

NAVY, ARMY & AIRFORCE BOOKS PUBLISHED BY BREWIN BOOKS

World War I

From Mons to Messines	1 85858 148 6	£7.95
Kineton in The Great War: 1914-1921	1 85858 111 7	£8.95
Lest We Forget - Southam in the Great War	1 85858 216 4	£8.95
Letters from the Trenches	1 85858 163 X	£7.95
Remembering The Great War (Glouc & Here)	1 85858 226 1	£9.95

World War II

From Africa to the Arctic (R.N.)	1 85858 237 7	£6.95
Aegean Masquerade (R.A.F.)	1 85858 036 6	£7.95
Guns and Bugles (6th BN K.S.L.I.)	1 85858 192 3	£15.95
Hospital Ship - Naval Memoirs (R.N.)	1 85858 197 4	£8.95
How was it for you? (British Legion)	1 85858 210 5	£9.95
Mars and Venus (Worcs Yeomanry)	1 85858 160 5	£4.95
Raiders Past: Air Raids Over Yardley	1 85858 019 6	£5.95
Shadow Over Our Days - Occupied France	1 85858 122 2	£6.95
Shadow Over Our Days - (French Edition)	1 85858 139 7	£6.95
Somewhere in The Midlands (U.S.)	1 85858 119 2	£6.95
They Also Serve - Who Stand and Wait (U.S.)	1 85858 204 0	£9.95
A Trenchard Brat - A Life in Aviation (R.A.F.)	1 85858 152 4	£17.95
Wartime Worcestershire	1 85858 058 7	£7.95
We'll Meet Again (Service Memories)	1 85858 172 9	£7.95

National Service

Erk's Eye View - R.A.F. National Service	1 85858 054 4	£7.95

The Falkland Islands War

The Falklands Watcher	1 85858 140 0	£12.95